CREATIVE READING
FOR GIFTED LEARNERS
a design for excellence
second edition

Michael Labuda, *Editor*

Jersey City State College

Published by the
International Reading Association
800 Barksdale Road, Box 8139, Newark, Delaware 19714

INTERNATIONAL READING ASSOCIATION

OFFICERS
1985-1986

President John C. Manning, University of Minnesota, Minneapolis, Minnesota

Vice President Roselmina Indrisano, Boston University, Boston, Massachusetts

Vice President Elect Phylliss J. Adams, University of Denver, Denver, Colorado

Executive Director Ronald W. Mitchell, International Reading Association, Newark, Delaware

DIRECTORS

Term Expiring Spring 1986
Marie M. Clay, University of Auckland, Auckland, New Zealand
Dale D. Johnson, University of Wisconsin, Madison, Wisconsin
Barbara M. Valdez, North Sacramento School District, Sacramento, California

Term Expiring Spring 1987
Carl Braun, University of Calgary, Calgary, Alberta, Canada
Nora Forester, Northside Independent School District, San Antonio, Texas
Susan Mandel Glazer, Rider College, Lawrenceville, New Jersey

Term Expiring Spring 1988
P. David Pearson, University of Illinois, Champaign, Illinois
Margaret Pope, North Little Rock, Arkansas
Carol M. Santa, School District #5, Kalispell, Montana

Copyright 1985 by the
International Reading Association, Inc.

Library of Congress Cataloging in Publication Data
Main entry under title:

Creative reading for gifted learners, second edition.

    Includes bibliographies.
    1. Gifted children—Education—Reading—Congresses.
I. Labuda, Michael. II. International Reading Association.
LC3993.5.C73 1985   371.95'3   85-10789
ISBN 0-87207-742-X

CONTENTS

Foreword *v*
Introduction *vii*

PART ONE CREATIVE PUPILS AND CREATIVE READING

2 Gifted and Creative Pupils: Reasons for Concern **Michael Labuda**
8 Rationale for Fostering Creative Reading in the Gifted and the Creative **Paul A. Witty**
26 Ingredients of a Creative Reading Program **Walter B. Barbe**

PART TWO SPECIAL CONSIDERATIONS

34 Parent Roles in Fostering Reading **Edith H. Grotberg**
46 Language Programs for Young Children: Implications for the Creative and Gifted **Dorothy S. Strickland**
51 Using Reading to Stimulate Creative Thinking in the Intermediate Grades **Richard J. Smith**
60 Creativity in Secondary Schools **Jo Brazell**

PART THREE MATERIALS AND RESOURCES

70 Fostering Reading Growth for Gifted and Creative Readers at the Primary Level **Carl J. Wallen**
80 Fostering Creative Reading at the Intermediate Level **Robert E. Shafer**
97 Creativity Training Activities for Secondary School Students **Joseph S. Renzulli** and **Carolyn M. Callahan**

PART FOUR MEETING WRITING NEEDS

106 Writing as Revelation: From Telephone Booth to Macrocosmic View **Michael Mathias**

PART FIVE   SUGGESTIONS FOR MEETING UNIQUE NEEDS

122   Make Believe: An Important Affair   **Margaret S. Woods**

133   Creative Reading Can Be a Balance and an Anchor in Guiding the Gifted   **Ann F. Isaacs**

145   Fostering Creativity in Children Who Differ   **Michael Labuda** and **Helen J. James**

PART SIX   A LOOK AHEAD

160   Forging Ahead in Reading for Gifted and Creative Learners   **Michael Labuda**

166   The Twenty-First Century   **Michael Labuda**

170   Organizations for the Gifted

IRA PUBLICATIONS COMMITTEE 1985-86   Martha D. Collins, Louisiana State University, *Chair* • Janet R. Binkley, IRA • Richard L. Carner, University of Miami • Nicholas P. Criscuolo, New Haven, Connecticut, Public Schools • Richard C. Culyer III, Coker College • James E. Flood, San Diego State University • Michael P. French, Beaver Dam Unified School District, Wisconsin • Susan Mandel Glazer, Rider College, *Board Liaison* • Philip Gough, University of Texas at Austin • Pearl Grubert, Protestant School Board of Greater Montreal, Montreal, Quebec • Ruby W. Martin, Tennessee State University • Ronald W. Mitchell, IRA • Lesley M. Morrow, Rutgers University • María Elena Rodríguez, IRA, Buenos Aires • Robert Schreiner, University of Minnesota • Jennifer A. Stevenson, IRA.

The International Reading Association attempts, through its publications, to provide a forum for a wide spectrum of opinion on reading. This policy permits divergent viewpoints without assuming the endorsement of the Association.

FOREWORD

Individual differences have long been a focus of reading research and a major concern for teaching practice. Most of us agree that the question of what it is to read with understanding is a highly complex issue. We also agree that numerous social and personal factors affect reading skill and achievement. Understanding both the complexity of the task and the uniqueness of the individual becomes a complicated matter. Many researchers have moved toward the study of complex cognitive processes, and, for years, there have been practicing teachers who recognize talented students in their classrooms and feel they must develop special programs for those learners.

Gifted learners and creative people are our most valued natural resource. Given a stimulating and enriching educational experience, these students will provide the major leadership for tomorrow's world but, as teachers know, these are students who are frequently "turned off" by normal progression through a standard curriculum. In a social climate when everyone seems to be demanding "excellence" in schools, it is appropriate for us to look closely now at the needs of this special group of students.

Reading is an area in which gifted and creative students seem to excel. Reports of early reading by gifted children are commonplace. Similarly, reports of the childhoods of creative individuals often include accounts of extensive reading. Moreover, we know that gifted and creative individuals have little patience for drill and routine. Each of these factors has implications for reading teachers, and it is fitting that the issues be addressed by the International Reading Association.

A vast body of research has been amassed on the processes of critical and creative reading. This kind of reading embodies higher level thinking, and involves filling gaps, making connections, and solving problems. It also embraces a level of sensitivity to the subtleties of language and literature not possessed by the typical student. While many researchers have reinterpreted these capabilities as response to literature, the definitions of critical and creative reading noted here continue to carry meaning for classroom teachers.

The editor and authors of this book recommend creative reading for gifted learners. They address the issues and problems of identifying this special population of learners, and define the process of creative reading. They illustrate a number of language, reading, and writing programs which are suitable for gifted learners at various ages. They point out the role that parents must play in fostering reading, and identify numerous resources needed to meet the unique needs of gifted students. Indeed, the need for a second edition of *Creative Reading for Gifted Learners* has been well met.

Bernice E. Cullinan
New York University

INTRODUCTION

It is the intent of this volume to indicate both the nature of children who possess traits of giftedness and creativity and the comprehensive educational procedures required to meet their needs.

Part One attends to two elements: the characteristics of gifted and creative children and an explication of a creative reading program. Labuda gives an overview of the reasons for concerns about gifted and creative learners. The summary of research by Witty (updated by Labuda) highlights the needs of gifted children and the meaning of creative reading. Barbe explains the scope of a creative reading program, including the goals, resources and materials, and skills taught.

Part Two covers important aspects of creativity and creative reading for teachers to consider as they implement instructional programs. Grotberg presents views of home and parent influences on gifted children and describes how parents and teachers may work together to provide for these children. Strickland delineates the elements of a total language arts program for young children (K-3), substantiating the need for oral language development as a foundation for reading skills development. Smith discusses reading as a thinking process and then outlines the special characteristics and reading needs of intermediate grade children, concluding with suggestions for meeting needs that may be relevant to educational programs at all levels. The problems of secondary pupils are reviewed by Brazell, followed by some solutions for gifted and creative students. Teachers of the middle school grades (6-9) will find a wealth of suggestions for individualization of their classroom programs in the articles by Smith and Brazell.

Part Three proposes specific materials and resources that have fostered reading growth for pupils in grades K-12. Wallen describes reading goals, materials, and skills for primary grade children; the review of current approaches will enable teachers to select ideas suitable for their own programs. Shafer explains ways to give intermediate grade pupils a broad program involving the total language arts; teachers of grades 5-8 will find many ideas for improvement of pupils' total communication skills. Renzulli and Callahan postulate four principles underlying creativity training of secondary pupils; they then explain training activities that will enable older youths to produce creatively.

Part Four proposes dramatized writing across the curriculum. Mathias describes a hierarchy of five principles of thought in which many different kinds of knowledge are offered for developing prewriting, writing, and editing in an integrated curriculum. In his circular model for meaning across the curriculum he cites students' examples, suggesting how readers can play a much more active-constructive role in their own comprehension.

Part Five gives attention to the unique needs of certain gifted and creative children. Woods urges teachers to capitalize on children's natural tendency to "make-believe" and demonstrates ways to enhance the growth of children's imaginative solutions to problems. Isaacs details the needs of gifted children as they cope with their own uniqueness in what is largely a conforming environment; after reviewing a variety of general approaches that provide guidance to such children in and through reading activities, she concludes the chapter with an extensive list of enriching activities. Labuda and James examine the needs of minority group children and learning disabled children who give evidence of giftedness or creativity and propose educational implications for these children, concluding with examples of creative production by children who differ in multiple ways.

In Part Six, Labuda appropriately concludes the volume with a glimpse of encouraging trends and offers suggestions for needs in the future.

Helen J. James

Note from the Editor: Because of the enthusiastic response from teachers and students, much of the second edition of Creative Reading for Gifted Learners *remains the same. The material remains relevant, although we use some different terms and expressions today. However, in most instances, the chapters were updated or revised.*

PART ONE
CREATIVE PUPILS AND CREATIVE READING

This section provides the reader with the basic *rationale* for a concern about improving reading instruction for gifted and creative learners. The focus is on two elements: defining the gifted and creative learner and defining creative writing.

The topics have been sequenced to furnish a sound foundation for curriculum adaptation. A general overview presents the basic problem; evidence from research supports the premise that there are gifted and creative pupils of diverse nature and that creative reading can play an important role in providing for the needs of these pupils. The considerable documentation provided in these chapters attempts to demonstrate the value of a creative reading program for the gifted and to provide arguments for special reading instruction for talented learners in each classroom.

ML

GIFTED AND CREATIVE PUPILS: REASONS FOR CONCERN

Michael Labuda
Jersey City State College

Interest in special educational programs for the gifted and creative is not new. Greatness in human existence, aspiration, and achievement is a theme which has been treated since prehistoric times in literature and art and more recently through scholarly analysis and research. Throughout history, recognition and encouragement have definitely depended upon the nature of the gift and the cherished beliefs of the time. However, at all times, including the present, provisions have been unsystematic and inadequate.

The earliest definition of gifted children was based on objective criteria and was stated in terms of IQ derived from an intelligence test. Later, to acknowledge creative behavior, the definition most commonly accepted was one in which consistently remarkable performance was achieved in any potentially valuable area. More recently the advisory panel to the U.S. Commissioner of Education established the following definition for the purpose of Federal education programs (1).

> Gifted and talented children are those by virtue of outstanding abilities capable of high performance. These are children who require differentiated educational programs and/or services beyond those normally provided by the regular school program in order to realize their contribution to self and society.
>
> Children capable of high performance include those with demonstrated achievement and/or potential ability in any of the following areas, singly or in combination:
>
> 1. general intellectual ability
> 2. specific academic aptitude
> 3. creative or productive thinking
> 4. leadership ability
> 5. visual and performing arts

It can be assumed that utilization of these criteria for identification of the gifted and talented will encompass a minimum of 3 to 5 percent of the school population.

Evidence of gifted and talented abilities may be determined by a multiplicity of ways. These procedures should include objective measures and professional evaluation measures which are essential components of identification.

Professionally qualified persons include such individuals as teachers, administrators, school psychologists, counselors, curriculum specialists, artists, musicians, and others with special training who are also qualified to appraise pupils' special competencies.

The advisory panel cautions the use of an operational definition which is too specific and does not allow for flexibility. In its report to the U.S. Commissioner of Education, the panel offers an operational definition (1).

Generally, the following evidence would indicate special intellectual gifts or talent:

Consistently very superior scores on many appropriate standardized tests.

Judgment of teachers, pupil personnel specialists, administrators, and supervisors familiar with the abilities and potentials of the individual.

Demonstration of advanced skills, imaginative insight, and intense interest and involvement.

Judgment of specialized teachers (including art and music), pupil personnel specialists, and experts in the arts who are qualified to evaluate the pupil's demonstrated and/or potential talent.

Gifted and creative children at all levels are being denied the intellectual stimulation everyone deserves in a democratic society. These children will not triumph over mediocre education programs and achieve at a superior level without special assistance. According to the democratic tradition, the human being is the measure of all things and the all-powerful force in society. Mead (3) has called American culture a "fix-it" society in which whatever inferiorities people have demonstrated can be easily fixed. We have a colossal amount of faith that average or below average children can approximate the common person, while the gifted and creative—since they function above the common potential—are allowed to drift. This misfortune has resulted in an incalculable loss to society of leadership potential.

Gifted and creative children do exist outside our affluent society. In fact, among the greatest potential sources waiting are children whose gifts are disguised by clothing, dialect, or cultural differences.

From early childhood, gifted children give indications of superior intellectual ability. Typically half of the gifted have taught themselves to read, with some children reading as early as age two. These children may walk and talk at an earlier age than other children and in other ways indicate that they are advanced. Since they are more alert and learn more quickly, they are advanced in visual, auditory, language, and listening behavior skills.

Parents can share with the school an important responsibility in helping their children to achieve their maximum potential. They can read to their children; encourage originality; ask questions; provide a variety of experiences; nurture problem solving, curiosity, creativity and confidence; and demonstrate a love for reading by reading themselves. Once aware of their role, all parents, regardless of their socioeconomic levels, may stimulate the learning of their children.

The majority of researchers favor a continuous screening and search program. At the minimum, school must reevaluate students annually so that educational planning and placement will fulfill the educational needs of all gifted and creative children. Furthermore, in this search, there must be multiple measures of identification, including intelligence, achievement, talent, and creativity.

While the demonstrated and documented characteristics of the gifted and creative provide adequate information for planning educational experiences, little effort has been made to identify gifted and creative children at the preschool and elementary levels. In many instances, giftedness can be discerned in the preschool years. As children display signs of readiness for reading, teachers must be willing to accept their cues and begin to teach reading on the level at which the child may profit from the various procedures. In school systems where efforts have been made for them to satisfy their desires for knowledge and performance, there is a definite relationship between educational opportunities and adjustment. Those students who do surprisingly well were found to have the advantage of warm, stimulating, and supportive environments at home and in the school. Changes in curriculum, teacher behavior, and classroom organization are essential. All too often, however, the programs consist of one or two special classes, taken along with standard requirements.

A comparison of gifted and creative children with their age peers reveals that they have a longer attention span, a persistent curiosity, a desire to learn rapidly, a good memory, an awareness and appreciation of people and things, a wide range of interests, and the ability to solve the many problems besetting society. They value independence which is task and contribution oriented, reject conformity, hold high social ideals and values, and possess individuality and originality. Some in this group will need help in moving from primary reading habits to low maturity reading levels. Others are ready to read in a mature way with good speed and for a number of different purposes.

Exceptional capacities create problems for most people and for young children in particular. Since their ideas are advanced, these children sometimes do not fit into situations with others of their own age and find themselves marginal and isolated. However, since it is human to enjoy social association, the gifted and creative tend to relate to older companions and to games which involve individual skills or intellectual pursuits. This unique population has demonstrated the need for special programs to foster their unique abilities. Rather than less guidance, they need more guidance when compared to their peers. In good special programs, they have shown remarkable improvement in involvement and interest in learning. Many perform superbly in community groups, student government, and athletics. Their diverse pursuits require a balanced reading program which encompasses reading for many different purposes in many types of materials; e.g., they read for pleasure, for study in content areas, for classroom activities, for sharing ideas, and as a basis for creative activities. In the past, good programs on the secondary level have surpassed those being offered on the elementary levels.

Within recent years researchers have given increased attention to the topic of creativity. Many tests have been developed to measure creativity; presently there is considerable knowledge of the nature of the creative person, and creativity tests beyond the exploratory stages are available. It is depressing and almost inconceivable that 57.5 percent of all schools surveyed in a recent U.S. Office of Education survey reported having no gifted pupils (1). Whether the responses were the result of ignorance or apathy, clearly the gifted and creative have too few opportunities to develop to their fullest potential.

During the 70s gifted education embarked on an era of appropriate education for a diverse people in a diverse world. In the 80s the overall message of a "Nation at Risk" (4) is that gifted education will end and the quality of gifted educational programs will fail. Separate funding for gifted programs was eliminated by the federal government in 1981, resulting in additional cuts by state and local governments.

The National Commission on Excellence in Education and other studies have cited the critical importance of paying attention to education of the gifted in our society. We must have sufficient numbers of scientists, engineers, and technicians emerging from our nation's schools to insure competent brainpower to compete in the future. Although we have only identified one-half of the estimated 2.5 million gifted children in this country, and only 16 states require certification for teachers of the gifted, a rekindling of public and political awareness has emerged. Polls indicate that the public wants equal funding for gifted, and legislators have introduced sizeable appropriation bills in Congress.

Today, teachers are provided with numerous new and exciting instructional materials that encourage growth. However, materials must be at an appropriate level of difficulty for each individual. The determination of a program should be based upon the needs of particular children in each individual situation. Students will be led to the fullest development of their abilities only if teachers use materials in relation to the needs of each individual. Even with traditional materials, gifted and creative pupils can be challenged to grow when assignments are based on achievement levels.

The reading needs of the gifted and creative differ in many respects from those of other groups; indeed, needs are different for each child within each group. The gifted child can develop to the maximum if taught to think and act in a creative manner. Strict regimentation does not create an atmosphere conducive to creative thinking and creative reading. The child must be encouraged to express ideas freely and not feel restrained because of nonconformity or divergent thinking. This can best be accomplished in a classroom atmosphere of freedom—freedom which permits the child to learn at an individual level and rate. Perhaps teachers need to think in terms of encouraging tomorrow's minds rather than yesterday's minds, giving children freer range to focus on the unsolved part of the curriculum, rather than only on the solved parts. We need to implant enough knowledge to cause children to think and then encourage them to expand their understanding through unaccustomed avenues of intellectual activity. Since the gifted may become zealous readers with many special interests, free access to many supplementary materials should be provided. Interests will expand through exposure to interesting ideas, activities, and materials. A number of processes, abilities, and purposes will be employed and undoubtedly will soon embrace many different skills, concepts, and attitudes.

SUMMARY

A reorientation of public attitude concerning education of the gifted and creative child from all socioeconomic levels must take on a new impetus. Myths must be demolished regarding the ideas that gifted children need less guidance, will triumph over mediocre programs, and come only from affluent society. The extension of opportunities to the gifted is not undemocratic; in a democratic society we must provide opportunities for all gifted and creative children so that they may be permitted to grow to their fullest capacity.

In general, the research and literature on reading instruction support the idea that gifted and creative pupils can attain the highest level of ability—that of evaluative and creative behavior—if they gain the skills that make them independent. From early age to adulthood, maximum growth in reading and study skills is not only desirable but essential for them.

The needs of gifted and creative students are evident; they deserve the best and most fulfilling educational experiences we can offer. They deserve programs characterized by balance and breadth and which offer an opportunity for specialization in line with children's interests at all levels. By extending and enriching opportunities in reading, educators can take a significant step forward in providing the kind of education the gifted so justly deserve; the kind of education that will enhance their growth and the fulfillment of their potential.

References
1. *Education of the Gifted and Talented.* Report to Congress by the U.S. Commissioner of Education and background papers submitted to the U.S. Office of Education. Washington, D.C.: U.S. Government Printing Office, 1972. (72-502 0)
2. Marland, Sidney P., Jr. "Our Gifted and Talented Children: A Priceless National Resource," *Intellect,* October 1972.
3. Mead, Margaret, "The Gifted Child in American Culture Today," *Journal of Teacher Education,* 5 (September 1954).
4. National Commission on Excellence in Education. *A Nation at Risk.* Washington, D.C.: U.S. Government Printing Office, 1983.

RATIONALE FOR FOSTERING CREATIVE READING IN THE GIFTED AND THE CREATIVE*

Paul A. Witty

IDENTIFICATION OF GIFTED AND CREATIVE PUPILS

After the widespread use of intelligence tests, attention in our schools centered on the range of abilities within every classroom and the need for adaptations and extensions of the curriculum to care for the individual differences. Special provisions were made for slow learning pupils, and efforts were undertaken occasionally to enrich the experiences of the gifted (5,31).

Initial Research Efforts

The gifted child was generally considered to be one of high IQ, a conviction that long continued in education. Comprehensive studies of Lewis M. Terman, following the pioneer work of Alfred Binet, led to the testing of large numbers of children and youth and to assignment of children to various categories of ability. Children earning IQs of 130 and higher, designated as gifted, constituted about one percent of elementary school pupils in the early surveys, while somewhat higher percentages were later reported. Pupils with IQs of 140 and higher were assigned to the category "genius" or "near genius."

Large scale genetic investigations of the gifted were made about 1920. Reports of these studies were published in several volumes and were summarized by Terman and Oden. Terman (21) stated that the following findings were most significant:

> Children of IQ 140 or higher are, in general, appreciably superior to unselected children in physique, health, and social adjustments; markedly superior in moral attitudes as measured either by character tests or by trait ratings; and vastly superior in their mastery of school subjects as shown by a three-hour battery of achievement tests. In fact, the typical child of the

*This chapter was reviewed and updated by Michael Labuda in memory of Paul A. Witty.

group had mastered the school subjects to a point about two grades beyond the one in which he was enrolled, some of them three or four grades beyond.

Follow-up investigations were made over a period of 40 years. These studies showed that the academic superiority of the gifted pupil was maintained and that "the promise of youth" was realized to a conspicuous degree insofar as superiority in school was concerned. Most of these individuals actually improved their relative status on mental ability test scores in adulthood. Thus, Terman stated:

> Close to 90 percent entered college and 70 percent graduated. Of those graduating, 30 percent were awarded honors and about two-thirds remained for graduate work.

Further investigations of the gifted as young adults, compared with studies of proven geniuses, convinced Terman that:

> The genius who achieves the highest eminence is one whom intelligence tests would have identified as gifted in childhood.

Researchers have differed sharply in the interpretation of the data. Is it feasible to justify IQ solely on genetic nature without any inclusion of environmental intervention? Although the results of Witty's studies of gifted children agreed closely with those of Terman, he differed sharply in the interpretation of the data. He questioned whether one is justified in assuming that a high IQ may be used to predict creative behavior or the achievements of the genius. Moreover, he emphasized the importance of factors such as interest, drive, opportunity, and early education in affecting the nature and extent of individual attainment.

Clearly, these studies of gifted pupils demonstrated the value of the IQ in selecting one type of child for whom promise of academic attainment is great and for whom appropriate opportunities are needed. It became clear that enrichment of various kinds was beneficial in both the elementary and the secondary school. However, the amount of such provisions has been, and continues to be, meager.

Recognition of the Importance of Early Learning

Terman and his associates emphasized the importance of hereditary factors in producing relatively stable IQs. Although these investigators mentioned the significance of opportunities for early learning, their studies of the gifted dealt largely with pupils of school age after early childhood had passed.

Recently, the importance of the early years has been brought vividly to our attention. Research has shown that early admission practices do not have negative effects for students. Many gifted children are ready for structured learning experiences as early as age four. Thus, Pines (15) has stated:

> Millions of children are being irreparably damaged by our failure to stimulate them intellectually during their crucial years—from birth to six. Millions of others are being held back from their true potential.

Undeniably, intellectual stimulation for young children has been neglected, not only in the home but in the nursery school or preschool center (34). It is being asserted that the provision of rich and varied experiences in early childhood will increase learning ability and heighten intelligence. It is believed that a more general provision of such opportunities would raise the incidence of superior children residing in areas in which deprivation and disadvantage prevail.

Findings Concerning Children Who Read Early

Investigators have recently stressed the potential of children for learning to read at early ages. The possibility was long ago recognized by scholars who suggested that perhaps age four was the time most desirable for beginning reading instruction. It was proposed that reading instruction be started earlier, but opposition was great since most educators believed that children needed a mental age of six years or more before they were ready for reading instruction. In 1966, Durkin's study (8) of children who read early caused many thoughtful people to reexamine this issue. Durkin reported that children in a group, one-third of whom had IQs below 110, entered the first grade with superior achievement in reading and maintained their lead over a five year period. Notable was Durkin's description of the parents of the early readers. They were characterized as having respect for learning and supporting its encouragement in very young children.

In a study of seven year olds who read before entering school, Clark (6) reported findings similar to Durkin's. Children were able to decode unusual words out of context and apparently used contextual clues in oral and silent reading to increase fluency and comprehension.

The need for early intervention was also supported by the Seattle Project longitudinal study (18). This preschool program provided an optimal match between educational programing and each child's level of competence in various subject areas while nurturing intellectual, social, emotional, and physical growth.

Social scientists at ETS (*17*) reported on a six year study of more than a thousand children from low income families of varied academic achievement. They found that those children who had the advantage of a warm, stimulating, and supportive environment at home and in school did surprisingly well.

In studies (*32, 33*) at Northwestern University, the parents of gifted children who read early appeared to be similarly concerned about their children's achievement during the early crucial years. These parents frequently read aloud to their children, fostered language expression, provided varied books and materials, and showed by their own behavior a respect for reading. Some of these parents encouraged their children to write, spell, and record their experiences in simple forms. Under these conditions, more than half of the gifted group learned to read, without undue pressure, before starting school.

Identification of the Creative Pupil

Two fundamental views for approaching the nature of creativity are prevalent. One is approached through the use of a set of teachable cognitive skills and cognitive models. The other approach views personality traits such as risk taking, independence, humor, and a strong self-concept as setting the creative apart from their peers.

The use of standard intelligence measures will not enable one to identify the creative pupil with great success. The creative individual commonly has a relatively low IQ, and therefore, the correlation between IQ and highly creative performance is low. Intelligence tests measure convergent thinking and evaluation while creativity is reflected by divergent thinking abilities. Materials generally used in intelligence tests are not suited for eliciting novel, imaginative, or creative responses. Undoubtedly, the intelligence test has helped in the identification of one kind of ability, but it does not enable one to identify creative pupils accurately.

Getzel and Jackson (*9*) found that the average score on standardized achievement tests for students exceptionally high in creativity (but not in IQ) and those exceptionally high in IQ (but not in creativity) were equal. However, teachers preferred high IQ gifted since they tend to be less abrasive in the classroom. The work of Guilford (*11*) has stimulated a prolonged search for the components of creativity with attention to factors such as sensitivity to problems, fluency, flexibility, and originality. Torrance (*23*) developed a series of creative tests that consider a wide range of abilities in identification and program development. Many other tests of creativity are listed in a compendium by Biondi and Parnes (*3*). Although critics have cited caution in using tests of creativity, these tests may identify children not picked up by other means, particularly minority students who may be at a disadvantage on other kinds of tests.

Search for a Variety of Creative Abilities

Despite the limitation of tests of creativity, one may recognize a number of practical approaches in the identification of children whose promise of creativity is great. For example, Witty (*30*) reported on a creative writing study in which he used a film with a musical score and background sounds but no commentary. After viewing the film, pupils were asked to write a commentary, story, or poem about the film. Approximately 10 percent of the pupils wrote so effectively that their products suggested unique creative ability as judged by three experts who examined the work to select compositions of creative superiority and qualitative excellence. The agreement of these judges was close in regard to the top creative pupils. Moreover, in several analyses, if only a high IQ had been used to identify the gifted, a large number of the top creative pupils would have been excluded. Many of the outstanding compositions were written by pupils who had not previously been observed as having unusual aptitude in writing. If additional outstanding performance corroborated this first demonstration of exceptional ability, these pupils would be considered potentially gifted in this area (*29, 30*).

Because of such findings, Witty proposed that a potentially gifted child be considered any child whose performance in a worthwhile type of human endeavor is repeatedly or consistently remarkable. He suggested that a search be made, not only for pupils of high verbal ability, but also for those of unusual promise in mathematics and sciences, writing, art, music, drama, mechanical ability, and social leadership.

Scholars are increasingly recognizing the prevalence of undiscovered talent and are initiating a quest for multiple talents in children and youth. Different multitalent types of gifted educational programs are being provided in many existing programs. This is particularly common where large populations are involved, such as Chicago and New York City. Successful summer Governors' programs in Georgia, North Carolina, and other states have effectively employed approaches to find and further develop creativity in pupils. In addition, the Johns Hopkins University and Duke University programs find and nurture students with unusual mathematical and linguistic talents.

Social Adjustments of Gifted and Creative Pupils

We have already noted the characteristics of some gifted children who have been identified by intelligence tests. In addition to their superiority in school work, the high IQ children were found typically to be well-adjusted socially and to get along well with their peers. Creative pupils were found typically to be less well-adjusted and to have difficulties in peer relationships. Thus, Torrance (24) states:

> Many of the highly creative individuals are disturbing elements in classroom groups in elementary schools. The problem of teachers and guidance workers resolves itself into one of helping highly creative individuals maintain those characteristics which seem essential to the development of creative talent and, at the same time, helping them acquire skills for avoiding, or reducing to a tolerable level, the peer sanctions.

The findings of Torrance are supported in a study by Victor and Mildred G. Goertzel (10). These authors chose 400 persons, acknowledged as eminent by a high frequency of biographies currently written about them. Concerning their childhood, the authors state:

> They showed their greatest superiority in reading ability; many read at the age of four. Almost all were early readers of good books. They were original thinkers and had scant patience with drill and routine. They were likely to be rejected by their playmates and had parents who valued learning.

The authors indicate also that "Three out of five of the four hundred had serious school problems" and conclude:

> Now as in the days of the Four Hundred, the child who is both intelligent and creative remains society's most valuable resource. When we learn to work with him instead of against him, his talents may reward us in ways beyond our ability to imagine.

Recommendations for Reading Instruction of the Gifted

The evidence of research makes clear some of the characteristics of gifted and creative pupils. In terms of these characteristics the following practices in reading instruction and guidance appear to be worthy of implementation.

1. The guidance of the reading of the gifted child should begin at home. Gifted children who are able to read on entering school have parents who often read aloud to them and patiently answer questions about words. Their homes sometimes contain children's magazines, picture and story books, dictionaries, and encyclopedias. The parents themselves turn to reading for information and pleasure (28). Some are particularly interested in providing a stimulating environment and in encouraging learning during the crucial early years.

2. Some gifted pupils are able to read on entering kindergarten and they should be given opportunities to apply and develop their reading

abilities. Those gifted children who are not able to read on entering school should be offered a broad background of first-hand experience coupled with varied forms of language expression. They should be encouraged to decode, pronounce, write, and spell words which appear in their own experience charts. If gifted children are able to read on entering first grade, they should be encouraged to do so from varied sources that are individually suitable and appealing. They should not be limited to typical, routine basal instruction and unnecessary readiness activities. Emphasis should be placed on reading as a thinking and communicating process (30).

3. Varied approaches may be used in the initial reading instruction of the gifted. An effective way to introduce children to reading as a thinking process is to have them tell a story depicted by pictures of a familiar incident arranged in sequence. The pupils may then be encouraged to tell stories from picture books devoid of text. Reading may be appreciated further as a way of communicating in activities such as the "reading" of faces, signs, and illustrations (25). Children's own words may then be recorded in their own stories and used as their first reading material. Teachers who follow the language experience approach encourage children to make their own books as initial reading material. Experience charts are widely employed by others. Individualized reading instruction may also foster the use of self-selection and pacing in reading. Gifted children will read books on a variety of topics and will find satisfaction in sharing their discoveries in reading with their classmates. Under these conditions, gifted children's ability and interest develop rapidly. By the time they reach fourth grade, they usually have become avid readers.

4. The teacher who seeks to enrich the reading experience of the gifted child within the regular classroom has a special problem. Witty (28) has described successful efforts of teachers to deal with the problem created by the wide range of ability within the typical classroom. In such classrooms, the results of interest inventories may be used to set up small flexible reading groups to explore topics of interest. Reading materials related to each topic may be made available on varied levels of difficulty. Gifted pupils may make their contributions from reading the more advanced subject matter on each topic. This strategy is being used effectively in subject areas such as science or social studies.

5. The importance of interests should be fully recognized. Studies have shown that most gifted children have rich and varied interests in which reading can readily be related; however, some gifted pupils have few wholesome interests. In these cases, efforts should be made to cre-

ate new patterns of interest though direct experience, the use of films and filmstrips, and other activities. Some gifted children concentrate their reading in a single specialized area such as science. Others make little use of varied types of reading materials. Teachers and librarians should work together to assist such pupils balance their reading. Here again, the interest inventory may be useful.

6. Gifted and creative students clearly need reading experiences that will help them meet their personal and social problems with success. In this effort, narratives and biographies have proved helpful. Although such pupils may not always benefit by reading alone, reading has proved beneficial, particularly when it is accompanied by discussion and relevant experiences.

7. Gifted children should be encouraged to enjoy poetry, an area they sometimes neglect. Anthologies of poetry such as Untermeyer's *Golden Treasury of Poetry* (Golden, 1969), Fisher's *Out in the Dark and Daylight* (Harper, 1980), Larrick's *Piper, Pipe that Song Again* (Random, 1965), Silverstein's *Where the Sidewalk Ends* (Harper, 1974), and *A Light in the Attic* (Harper, 1982) are favorites. Children should be given opportunities not only to read poetry, but also to write poetry. In many innovative programs for the gifted, creative writing is featured as a correlate to reading; strategies such as the use of unfinished stories, the writing of *Haiku, Cinquain,* and *Tanka,* and other techniques motivate creative expression (*30, 34*).

MEETING THE NEEDS OF GIFTED AND CREATIVE PUPILS: THE ROLE OF CREATIVE READING

Some scholars believe that a great stimulus in the education of the gifted would result from the general inauguration of a program of creative reading (*7, 25*). One may think of reading in two ways: The first stresses pronunciation and simple comprehension through the accurate identification of words and thought units. Creative reading, the second way, may be regarded as the highest and most neglected aspect of reading (*19, 25*).

In the first type of reading, exercises requiring study of the meanings of words and phrases in context help establish accurate perception, thus helping readers appreciate the literal meaning of passages. Emphasis on skills such as getting the central thought of a paragraph or noting details is relevant in this endeavor. This practice also involves the pupil's sensing the relationships of the material or ideas to previous experience. These assimilative responses will include widely varied reactions because of the greatly differing backgrounds of pupils. The reactions are, to a considerable degree, "convergent" in nature. Only to a small degree do they extend beyond the facts presented, and constitute "divergent production" (25).

We may consider creative reading a thinking process in which new ideas are originated, evaluated, and applied. Divergent and varied responses, not right answers, are goals. Finally, the pupil evaluates conclusions reached and seeks to extend and use them.

Explanation of Creative Reading as a Process

Some advocates of creative reading, influenced by Guilford's writing (11) on the *Structure of Intellect,* stress mental operations such as cognition, memory, convergent production, divergent production, and evaluation.

Torrance (25) defines the foregoing operations as follows:

The first, *cognition,* includes discovery, awareness, recognition, comprehension, or understanding. The second, *memory,* refers to retention or storage, with some degree of availability, of information. Then there are two types of *productive thinking* in which something is produced from what has been cognized or memorized: *Divergent production* or the generation of information from given information, where emphasis is upon variety and quantity of output from the same source, and *convergent production* or the generation of information where emphasis is upon achieving unique or conventionally accepted best outcomes (the given information fully determines the response). The fifth operation is *evaluation,* reaching decisions or making judgments concerning the correctness, suitability, adequacy, desirability, and so forth of information in terms of criteria of identity, consistency, and goal satisfaction.

Students of creative reading frequently emphasize the significance of convergent and divergent production. Convergent production, as we have indicated, involves reading largely to obtain correct meanings; divergent production involves individual response, implying several possible answers, no single correct response, and novel, original, and imaginative reactions.

In his book, *Gifted Children in the Classroom,* Torrance states:

When a person reads creatively, he is sensitive to problems and possibilities in whatever he reads. He makes himself aware of the gaps in knowledge, the unsolved problems, the missing elements, things that are incomplete or out of focus. To resolve this tension, so important in the creative thinking process, the creative reader sees new relationships, creates new combinations, synthesizes relatively unrelated elements into a coherent whole, redefines or transforms certain pieces of information to discover new uses, and builds onto what is known.

Another approach to reading also stresses creative reading as a thinking process, but the approach is somewhat different from the Guilford emphasis. Russell (*19*) suggests that

...children, adolescents, and adults typically read at four overlapping levels, In ascending order these are
1. word identification
2. casual skimming
3. reading for exact, literal meanings
4. creative reading for
   a. implied and inferred meanings
   b. appreciative reactions
   c. critical evaluations

The first three types of reading are primarily efforts to assimilate the facts presented and their literal meaning. In word identification, the reader is concerned primarily about pronouncing each word successfully. The act involves not only phonetic and structural analysis but may also require the use of context clues in reading a passage accurately. At the second level, the reader skims to obtain general ideas or impressions, to find certain facts in a presentation, or even to decide whether to read a passage more carefully. This type of reading is often stressed in speed reading courses. Exact or literal meanings are sought in the next, more demanding level. Textbook assignments frequently require this type of literal reading. All three levels emphasize convergent reactions in which "right" answers are sought.

Creative reading, on the other hand, requires an active response which extends beyond the literal meaning. The first three levels of reading are involved, but the emphasis is on higher level responses and thinking (*19*). Creative reading resembles creative thinking in that the reader gains new insights by evaluating an hypothesis and reaching a conclusion. Thus, the creative reader goes beyond the facts and considers their meanings, implications, and usefulness (*19, 25*).

Russell (*19*) shows the following progression from the *convergent* (or correct answer) type to response of the higher *divergent* form:

Accurate perception of words and thought units
Understanding literal meanings
Integration of ideas with past experience
Seeing implied relationships, hidden meanings, reacting to symbols
Developing new ideas either appreciative or critical
Using these new ideas in other activities

Another approach to teaching reading as a thinking process is based on Bloom's *Taxonomy of Educational Objectives* (4), which classifies objectives in six categories. The classification is arranged according to the complexity of the operations as follows: knowledge, comprehension, application, analysis, synthesis, and evaluation. Jarolimek (12) uses this sequence in suggestions for teaching social studies skills:

> One large group of such skills deals basically with a variety of intellectual operations. Thinking, asking questions, using language, solving problems, interpreting stories and pictures, and making simple analyses are a few examples of skills of this type. In most cases, they are related to the informational content of the program. They do not deal basically with *getting* information but with interpreting, processing, and using information.

For teaching such social studies skills, Jarolimek recommends the use of questions which call for divergent responses, not correct answers.

In fostering creative reading generally, as in the cultivation of social studies skills, questions play an important role. In fact, Smith (20) points out that creative reading "could be taught best through the skillful use of questions." Moreover, he defines creativity "according to Bloom's (1956) delineation of the cognitive level of synthesis. Applied to reading, this means that ideas acquired from a reading selection are combined with ideas acquired elsewhere in a purposeful search for a new product, pattern, or structure.

Smith suggests that the expression of noncreative and creative responses may be prompted by "convergent questions" and by "divergent questions." He presents two lists labeled "Convergent Questions" and "Divergent Questions." A teacher following the first list would elicit noncreative responses (convergent) use of the second list would encourage creative responses (divergent). The somewhat modified lists follow:

Convergent Questions	Divergent Questions
1. Ask only for information that is in the story.	1. Ask for information not in the story.
2. Do not ask for the reader's personal ideas.	2. Ask for the reader's personal ideas.
3. Ask for a correct answer that can be determined by analyzing the story.	3. Evoke open-ended, inferred responses.
4. Focus on the author's meaning.	4. Focus on what the reader can add.

Guilford's three dimensional model has stimulated other models. Renzulli (16) in his *Enrichment Triad Model* suggests the use of general exploratory activities, group oriented training activities, and individual or small group investigations of real problems or topics by using appropriate methods of inquiry. Williams (27) presented a broad model to aid the teacher in modifying tasks in the classroom along the dimensions of subject matter content, pupil behavior, and strategies or modes of teaching. To stimulate higher thinking processes in young children, Woods (36) designed guides for developing the capacity of wonder through a sequence of arousing curiosity, spontaneous expression, recognizing creative communication, and encouraging research. There are many instructional modules on the market such as Taylor's "Multiple Talent Model," and Mary Meeker's "soi Sourcebooks." However, materials that are designed for and used in specific settings by specific teachers are much more effective.

The Role of the Teacher

The extent to which children develop creative abilities in reading depends largely upon their teacher. From the first, good teachers encourage children to question the facts they read rather than to accept them passively. Torrance (25) suggests:

Teachers can help children become creative readers in two major ways. First they can do things to help heighten the child's expectation and anticipation as a reading task is approached. Second, they can permit or encourage children to do something with what is read, either at the time it is read or afterwards.

The following procedures are helpful in promoting creative writing.

1. To provoke interest in creative reading from the start, a simple picture book story such as *May I Bring a Friend?* by Beatrice Shenk de Regniers may be employed. This funny fantasy is an ideal vehicle for encouraging children to react creatively and imaginatively. In the story, the king and queen have told a boy to bring his friends to tea. The boy has many animal friends. Which friends shall he bring? Told in verse, this delightful story may be used to encourage children to anticipate and check various outcomes depending on the animals they choose to go to the party. Children make suggestions from their own experiences, discuss outcomes, and check to determine the suitability of their choices as the progression of events unfolds.

2. Another helpful way to promote thinking responses is by the use of an inventory which contains a number of questions addressed to children about their interests. Young children, almost without exception, will report activities such as watching TV programs, enjoying animals, and playing

games. The range will be extensive and varied. Common interests may be ascertained and extended through reading. A readily accessible avenue for further enrichment of interests is available through the film or filmstrip. For example, the film *Three Little Kittens* may be shown to primary grade children interested in pets; the film presentation may be halted after the exciting viewing of the newborn kittens. The children may then be asked to discuss what will happen. What is to be done with the kittens? Thinking and speculation follow; finally, they watch the rest of the film and examine the film reader (D.C. Heath) to evaluate their guesses.

3. In history classes, sequences of events may be discussed in order, and at critical points the question "What do you think will happen now?" may be asked after the class has read a chapter silently, stopping just before a significant happening (*25*). Books may be closed and possibilities discussed. Later, the class can finish reading the chapter to ascertain what actually happened. Thus, we see how creative reading may be stimulated during the reading process. Follow-up activities assure elaboration or extension of what is read.

Follow-Up Activities

One of the simplest and most effective follow-up activities to employ after silent reading is to have children *read aloud* exciting stories and poems they have enjoyed. The children can use intonation, gesture, and movement to express pleasure, indignation, or surprise. The class or a particular child may retell a story and listen to it via tape or the magnetic sound track. Children may be encouraged to read materials with the thought in mind that they are to write a poem from a passage or make a book report in varied forms. They may also dramatize a story or devise a puppet play from an exciting part of the book. They can prepare scripts for movie, radio, or TV programs from books as well. Pupils may also extend and enrich their reading through the use of other media such as painting, singing, and dramatics.

Writing a new ending for a story or completing an unfinished story are other ways of extending reading in creative forms. For example, Witty (*35*) prepared for *Highlights for Children* magazine a short story entitled "The Cat in the Wall" which was based on a newspaper account about a child's beloved cat that disappeared. After some time, the cat's whereabouts were revealed when her meows resounded from one of the dining room walls. Attempts were made, to no avail, to entice the cat to come out. At last, the fire department was called and a hole was cut in the wall. As the family watched to see the cat pulled out of the wall, there was a meow at the front door. The story was stopped at this point and children were asked to submit endings telling how the cat got in and out of the wall. Many elaborated ingeniously on what they had read and revealed their ability to think in unique and imaginative ways. As Torrance (25) states:

> For the gifted child, however, work in elaborating what is read will have its greatest usefulness in developing the ability to relate the content of reading to previous knowledge, produce illustrations and applications, practice using what has been read, relate what has been read to other fields, and make associations that integrate reading into action.

Personal Discovery and Application through Reading

A good story may evoke questions and problems to be solved by additional reading. Thus, a gifted pupil was led to read and compare many long biographies of Thomas Jefferson after he had examined a provocative short story about Jefferson and his times. With the help of a librarian, he read widely about the accomplishments of this remarkable man. His discoveries caused him to make extensive personal plans and to remark, "Everyone should read about the many things this man did to make our country great. Each of us ought to be able to do something, especially when we realize what one man was able to do."

Another creative young reader was fascinated by a short biography of James Garfield and became a great admirer of this President who died at the hands of an assassin when he was very young. He sought to answer the question: What might this President have accomplished had he lived longer? In exploring this enticing topic the boy composed a provocative essay in which he projected the life of this gifted President into a future wherein he made many important contributions to solving pressing social problems and issues.

Critical Reading and Evaluation

Evaluation of what is read is one of the chief features of creative reading. The creative reader often has a purpose or goal for reading when starting to read. A question may, of course, arise during or after his reading.

Reading as a thinking process often involves an effort to answer questions and solve problems, a process in which the pupil formulates an hypothesis and seeks to verify conclusions.

Critical reading and creative reading are not always clearly differentiated. Critical reading is one aspect of creative reading; creative reading, however, is not always critical in nature. In reading a poem, a pupil may have an appreciative reaction, an emotional response which is largely uncritical in the usual sense. In such a case, the pupil may evaluate this response as to whether the joy or pleasure anticipated was experienced and whether the response was sufficiently rewarding to provoke seeking further satisfaction from similar experiences.

The critical reader may consider the author's background and competency for writing on the subject, and may also inquire about the author's freedom from bias and prejudice. Discovery of the limitations and prejudices of a writer may indeed become the chief goal of the pupil as he reads. Torrance (25) observes:

> Ferreting out the truth from what one reads requires that one be both a critical and a creative reader. Being a critical reader only makes a child aware of the biases and deficiencies in the accounts of writers. It takes a creative reader to understand the reasons behind discrepant accounts and reach sound conclusions about what is true.

The creative reader seeks sound conclusions, evaluates them, and makes valid decisions about their meaning and application.

PROGRAMS FOR CREATIVE READING

We believe that the experimental evidence from physiological and Gestalt psychology demonstrates children's capacity for insightful behavior and for thinking in early childhood. As a result of an examination of many studies, Russell (19) states:

> ...critical, creative reading is possible at all levels of the elementary school. Reasoning ability seems to begin at about three years of age and to develop gradually with experience and language. It develops continuously rather than appearing at fixed stages. There seems to be little difference in the way adults and children think, except that adults have a wider experience against which they may check their hypotheses and conclusions.

Gradually, school personnel are coming to accept the fact that children are capable of thinking and reasoning at early ages. Experiments have shown that insightful learning is possible in young children. Facts about children's learning during the early years (presented in books such as Maya Pines' *Revolution in Learning*) have caused many parents and teachers to recognize and accept the importance of cultivating intelligent response during the early years (15). Accordingly, creative reading programs are being initiated and the range and complexity of learning experiences are being extended for young children.

Advocates of creative reading are contributing to the improvement of instruction for junior-senior high school students by placing primary emphasis on reading as a part of a broad program in the humanities. For example, in Brockton, Massachusetts, the *Ceiling Unlimited* project is organized around the central theme of understanding humanity (*1*). In other programs, students seek solutions to broad social problems.

A popular approach at the junior high school level is described by Barbe and Renzulli (*1*). Critical reading and thinking constitute the major objectives of this program developed by the Great Books Foundation. Through the use of carefully developed discussion questions and materials, each pupil from the third grade to the twelfth is encouraged to examine "the material in a way that is significant in terms of his own background, capacity, attitude, and interest."

Thus we see an increased interest in innovative programs for the gifted and the creative student as well as a greater tendency to foster creative reading in some schools. We hope to see not only the expansion of such programs, but also that creative reading will be encouraged by teachers and practiced more frequently by students. For, as Toynbee (*26*) has written

> To give a fair chance to potential creativity is a matter of life and death for any society. This is all-important, because the outstanding creative ability of a fairly small percentage of the population is mankind's ultimate capital asset, and the only one with which only Man has been endowed.

SUMMARY

The gifted child is described according to traditional concepts based on early research which led to the designation of children of high IQ as gifted. The characteristics of such verbally gifted pupils are described. The creative pupil is also described in terms of recent research. Verbally gifted and creative pupils are then compared. It is shown that if a high IQ criterion is used to select the gifted, a majority of creative pupils might be missed. It is proposed that the gifted child be redefined as any pupil whose performance in a worthwhile type of human endeavor is consistently or repeatedly remarkable, thus making possible the inclusion of creative pupils in such areas as science and mathematics, music, art, writing, and social leadership. The validity of tests of creativity is also examined. It is proposed that work samples and other techniques in which pupils' gifts are judged by performance be used more widely in identifying the gifted. Illustrations are given of specific ways to elicit evidence of giftedness.

Creative reading is recommended for gifted pupils. This highest type of reading is considered to be a thinking process in which new ideas are originated, evaluated, and applied. Divergent and varied responses, not right answers, are goals as thinking transpires and conclusions are reached. Finally, the pupil evaluates conclusions and seeks to extend and use them. This concept is based upon the views presented by Torrance (25), Russell (12), and Jarolimek (9).

The presentation includes examples of ways the teacher may encourage creative reading in the classroom. Examples of programs to promote creative reading in our schools are also cited and creative reading and creative writing are viewed as parts of a desirable language arts approach for the gifted.

References
1. Barbe, Walter B., and Joseph Renzulli. "Innovative Programs for the Gifted and Creative," in Paul Witty (Ed.), *Reading for the Gifted and the Creative Student.* Newark, Delaware: International Reading Association, 1971.
2. Baskin, Barbara, and Karen H. Harris. *Books for the Gifted Child.* New York: R.R. Bowker, 1980.
3. Biondi, Angelo, and Sidney Parnes (Eds.). *Assessing Creative Growth.* Great Neck, New York: Creative Synergetic Associates, 1976.
4. Bloom, Benjamin S. et al. *Taxonomy of Educational Objectives,* Handbook I, Cognitive Domain. New York: Longmans-Green, 1956.
5. Bryan, J. Ned, and Lanora G. Lewis. "Are State Departments Failing to Provide for the Gifted?" *Accent on Talent,* 2 (May 1968).
6. Clark, Margaret M. *Young Fluent Readers.* London: Heinemann Educational Books, 1976.
7. DeBoer, John J. "Creative Reading and the Gifted Student," *Reading Teacher,* May 1963.
8. Durkin, Dolores. *Children Who Read Early.* New York: Teachers College Press, Columbia University, 1966.
9. Getzels, J.W., and P.W. Jackson. *Creativity and Intelligence.* New York: John Wiley and Sons, 1962.
10. Goertzel, Victor, and Mildred G. Goertzel. *Cradles of Eminence.* Boston: Little, Brown, 1962.
11. Guilford, J.P. "Potentiality for Creativity," *Gifted Child Quarterly,* 6 (Autumn 1962); "Structure of Intellect," *Psychological Bulletin,* 53 (1956).
12. Jarolimek, John. "Skills Teaching in the Primary Grades," *Social Education,* 31 (1967).
13. Passow, A. Harry (Ed.). *The Gifted and the Talented: Their Education and Development.* Part 1. The Seventy-Eighth Yearbook of the National Society for the Study of Education. Chicago: University of Chicago Press, 1979.
14. Polette, Nancy. *Picture Books for Gifted Programs.* Metuchen, New Jersey: Scarecrow Press, 1981.
15. Pines, Maya. *Revolution in Learning: The Years from Birth to Six.* New York: Harper and Row, 1967.

16. Renzulli, Joe. *The Enrichment Triad Model: A Guide for Developing Defensible Programs for the Gifted and Talented.* Mansfield Center, Connecticut: Creative Learning Press, 1977.
17. *Research and Development at ETS. The Quest for Equity.* Princeton, New Jersey: Educational Testing Service, 1981.
18. Roedell, Wendy, and Halbert Robinson. *Programming for Intellectually Advanced Preschool Children: A Program Development Guide.* Seattle, Washington: Child Development Research Group, University of Washington, 1977. (ED 151 094)
19. Russell, David. *Children Learn to Read* (2nd ed.). Boston: Ginn, 1961; *Children's Thinking,* Ginn, 1956.
20. Smith, Richard J. "Questions for Teachers—Creative Reading," *Reading Teacher,* February 1969. See also N. Sanders, *Classroom Questions—What Kinds?* New York: Harper and Row, 1966.
21. Terman, Lewis M. "The Discovery and Encouragement of Exceptional Talent," *American Psychologist,* 9 (June 1954).
22. Terman, Lewis M., and Melita H. Oden. "The Stanford Studies of the Gifted," in Paul A. Witty (Ed.), *The Gifted Child.* Boston: D.C. Heath, 1951.
23. Torrance, E. Paul. *Discovery and Nurturance of Giftedness in the Culturally Different.* Reston, Virginia: Council for Exceptional Children, 1977.
24. Torrance, E. Paul. "Explorations in Creative Thinking," *Education,* 81 (December 1960); "Are the Torrance Tests of Creative Thinking Biased Against or in Favor of Disadvantaged Groups?" *Gifted Child Quarterly,* Summer 1971.
25. Torrance, E. Paul. *Gifted Children in the Classroom.* New York: Macmillan, 1965.
26. Toynbee, Arnold. "Is America Neglecting Her Creative Minority?" *Accent on Talent,* 2 (January 1968).
27. Williams, Frank E. *Classroom Ideas for Encouraging Thinking and Feeling.* Buffalo, New York: D.O.K. Publishers, 1970.
28. Witty, Paul A. (Ed.) *Reading for the Gifted and the Creative Student.* Newark, Delaware: International Reading Association, 1971.
29. Witty, Paul A. (Ed.) "Contribution to the IQ Controversy from the Study of Superior Deviates," *School and Society,* 5 (April 20, 1940).
30. Witty, Paul A. "The Use of Films in Stimulating Creative Expression and in Identifying Talented Pupils," *Elementary English,* October 1956.
31. Witty, Paul A. *Helping the Gifted Child.* Chicago: Science Research Associates, 1952. (Revised with Edith H. Grotberg, 1970).
32. Witty, Paul A. "Reading for the Gifted," in J. Allen Figurel (Ed.), *Reading and Realism,* 1968 Proceedings, Volume 13, Part 1. Newark, Delaware: International Reading Association, 1969.
33. Witty, Paul A. "The Education of the Gifted and the Creative in the U.S.A.," *Gifted Child Quarterly,* Summer 1971.
34. Witty, Paul A. "Early Learning—A Crucial Issue," *Highlights for Teachers,* No. 13.
35. Witty, Paul A. "Fostering Creative Reading," *Highlights for Teachers,* No. 25.
36. Woods, Margaret. *Wonderwork: Creative Experiences for the Young Child.* Buffalo, New York: Dissemination of Knowledge, 1970.

INGREDIENTS OF A CREATIVE READING PROGRAM

Walter B. Barbe
Highlights for Children

Creative reading has not been given adequate attention by those concerned with how children learn. For this reason, it is important to examine those issues involved in developing a creative reading program.

Any discussion of creativity necessitates an examination of the terms frequently associated with it. For many years the label "gifted" was applied to children of high potential as well as those with high achievement. In more recent years, another aspect of human potential has come to be recognized as of equal importance to intelligence. This aspect has been labeled by many as "creative potential." Gifted children are viewed as those in a school setting, who have either achieved at a level considerably above that of their age group or given evidence of a potential to do so.

Creative children, however, are able to function in a manner different from that of the traditional and to produce or perform in new and innovative ways. Creativity implies that these individuals are not limited to seeking solutions in the traditional ways which they may have been taught. Instead, they view problems as being solvable and are able to free themselves from traditional bounds to seek solutions. While instruction may not produce giftedness, freedom to use the abilities which one has in ways other than traditional ones can result in creativity from each child in the classroom. If this freedom is provided, and if guidance is given creative reading will result.

GOALS OF READING INSTRUCTION

In general, the goal of reading instruction is the development of permanent skills and interests in reading. To assume that acquiring necessary word attack skills is enough is to oversimplify the task. Being able to call off words, without understanding and appreciation, is an almost meaningless exercise; knowing fewer words, and understanding and appreciating those known, appears to be more valuable.

The ultimate goal of reading instruction is to enable children to read for a variety of purposes (e.g., information, clarification, verification, pleasure, or escape). In addition, it is hoped that children will have the desire to read throughout their lives.

Creative readers are concerned with both the process and the results of reading. Too often reading instruction focuses solely on the process of reading or on the results of reading when *both* are of utmost importance. Interest in reading and enjoyment while reading are both parts of the process. Obtaining specific information is part of the result, as is completing a book for the purpose of being able to say one has read it. Creative reading is thus a complex endeavor involving both process and result.

For example, many people have enjoyed Edith Wharton's *Ethan Frome*. Yet the basis for this enjoyment is an almost morbid fascination in Ethan's tragic story and pathetic life. That one should get such pleasure from reading about another's misfortunes seems reprehensible and can confuse the reader as to what is pleasurable; but Wharton's style so involves readers in the process of reading and discovering Ethan's past that they are certain to say they have enjoyed the book.

For creative reading to occur, encouragement and instruction must come early in the learning-to-read process. For the teacher to believe that creative reading will occur at some later date when the child has mastered all of the basic skills of reading is a misconception of how learning occurs.

Kindergarten and first grade teachers need to be conscious of what creative reading is all about and need to provide situations in which children are rewarded for reading creatively. The instruction may be incidental in the early stages of reading instruction, but it should be planned and intentional throughout the elementary grades and should be an inherent part of any reading program at the secondary school level.

RESOURCES AND MATERIALS

It is to be assumed that teachers will use all resources and materials available in their classrooms, school, and community in the total educational program of developing children. Reading series, trade books, subject matter textbooks, and audiovisual aids are all expected to be part of the total instructional program. Special attention is directed here to some of the essential elements in a satisfactory program.

Libraries or Learning Centers

The library or learning center is the greatest asset which the teacher can use to promote creative reading. The teacher can develop creative reading to its fullest only with an abundance of material from which children may select what they want to read.

Readily accessible materials are a first step. This means that every classroom should have a library of materials pertaining to particular subjects or special interests. A home library, the contents of which change as children become older, is also be encouraged.

In addition to classroom and home libraries, there is still the utmost need for the school library. But the school library must be more accessible than it has frequently been in the past. The library needs to be a center not just for the bound book with the hard cover, but also for paperbacks, current magazines, newspapers, and up-to-date reference books.

Materials

Numerous sources promote creative reading. The traditional unfinished story found frequently in *Highlights for Children* is one such example. The children are asked to provide an ending to a story which may have many different endings, none of which is the correct one, for there is no single correct ending.

The motivation to read additional material may come from free discussion about material which a number of children have read. Such discussion may cause some children to reread material in a creative manner after gaining more insight into the topic.

Best Books in Print (Bowker) is an extensive listing of materials for children to read. Also recommended are the books on the American Library Association's list. *A Parent's Guide to Children's Reading* and *Teacher's Guide to Children's Reading* by Nancy Larrick (Doubleday) are both musts for any teacher who wants to encourage creative reading among children. The sixth edition of *Reading Ladders to Human Understandings,* edited by Eileen Tway (American Council on Education, in cooperation with the National Council of Teachers of English, 1982), categorizes books according to the problems currently facing children. The use of this reference can more easily promote involvement and identification on the part of children than any other action.

Use of Biographies

Bright children turn early to biographies. Frequently as early as the second grade, children of high ability will begin to select biographies in an attempt to identify with success. They have essentially mastered the basic skills of knowing how to read, have acquired critical reading skills, and have begun to acquire creative reading skills which require both projection and identification. The most obvious identification, of course, is that which occurs in a biography when readers associate themselves with characters who are ultimately successful. (One wonders whether the early introduction of biographies to children other than those of high ability might alter their self-concepts and their ultimate achievement.)

Teachers at any level must recognize the value of biographies. However, they must be cautioned against the selection of a single type, such as presidents of the United States. For identification to occur, the biography must be about a person with whom children *most* easily identify. Biographies of successful athletes and popular singers are abundant and should be available to children, along with other types of biographies.

Emphasizing the importance of identification to creative reading implies an issue on which there is currently much disagreement. Many people do not believe that children are influenced in their behavior by what they read. If this is true, then there seems to be little basis for a belief in creative reading. On the other hand, if children are influenced by what they read, then creative reading is indeed important in the development of self-concept, the establishment of lifestyle, and the ultimate success in assuming a responsible role in society. So that there is no misunderstanding, let me say that I strongly believe that the printed word influences behavior. The selection of material for children to read then becomes of utmost importance. Creative reading becomes more than merely reading beyond what the author intended; it actually becomes an element in the character and goal-setting development of each child.

REQUIRED SKILLS

Creative Reading Skills

Creative reading is the highest level of reading—higher even than critical reading. It is supposed by some that reading cannot be creative, for readers are limited by the thoughts and words of the author. This is untrue; persons who bring background and experiences to reading may then take from the reading selection far more than the author intended. An understanding of the author's motivation for writing a particular piece, and knowledge about the author's background and the circumstances in which the selection was written, aid readers in interpreting the material and also in achieving a unique view of a situation or an event as they integrate their and the author's experiences. To limit oneself to the literal meaning of the words which the author chose to use, or even to inferred meanings based on knowledge of the author's intentions, is to attain far less understanding than can result from creatively thinking about what is read.

Creative reading cannot exist without the presence of confidence in one's ability to read and understand the author's meaning; it also requires analysis, synthesis, and evaluation abilities associated with critical reading.

Teachers must be concerned with more than just traditional skills or traditional reading materials. Basal programs provide for a sequential development of skills, and the materials lend themselves to certain types of thinking activities which will promote creative reading; however, the possibilities are limited, and a wide range of other materials and resources are required to meet the needs of particular children at particular times.

Certain books do better lend themselves to creative reading at certain age levels because of their content and the author's writing skill. Teachers should always be on the lookout for such books. Perhaps the classic example for third grade children is *Charlotte's Web* by E.B. White. In this amazing book, children encounter new concepts and their reactions are inherently creative, for they respond in terms of their own unique makeup and not in some predetermined way.

The Suicide Mountains, a tale by John Gardner, can promote creative reading with gifted students. Gifted students, who are often misunderstood and stereotyped because they are gifted, identify readily with the three main characters, who would rather leap off the Suicide Mountains than give in to people who have stereotyped them according to their physical appearances. Gifted students can learn from the main characters not to be afraid.

Listening and Viewing Skills

The use of computers, films, filmstrips, recordings, photographs, and television programs must be promoted; training in all of the listening and viewing skills should be part of the program. Only if children view all of the many audiovisual materials available to them as aids to their creative reading can they be freed from the concept of reading as a limited activity confined to content found between the two covers of a single book.

Library Skills

Library skills are among the many skills needing further attention. This does not mean the traditional type of instruction which requires children to learn only how to locate different kinds of materials. Children must discover how to locate the names of important authors, facts about their lives, and sources where they can find out more about such people. They must be led to use many types of reference materials, compare a variety of sources, and understand the processes involved in locating various kinds of information. The advanced library skills will be learned easily and happily by children who have problems to solve, needs to meet, and interests to follow.

Recording Skills

Just as knowing how to find material is important, so is the ability to record what one wishes to express. Handwriting is an essential skill, and being able to write rapidly and legibly is important. Knowing how to use a typewriter is another valuable skill; there can be little justification in delaying instruction in the use of a typewriter much past the point of the child's attaintment of writing abilities. And children who know how to type can also easily learn to use computers, which can be valuable for recording, storing, and organizing information.

Notetaking and outlining skills must be developed within a framework of problem-solving. As children need to organize their ideas, they will need to learn shortcuts in producing written records. In some instances, they may need or want to learn minimal shorthand skills.

Creative Writing Skills

Creative reading and creative writing cannot be separated, for creative reading is dependent upon children's abilities to organize their creative interpretations and either record or report them. This is impossible if children are limited to rigid forms and to traditional reciting of facts. It is likely that creative writing instruction will precede high-level creative reading. The mechanical aspects of reproducing one's thoughts as well as the importance of spelling and legible handwriting must be minimized, as children first grapple with the problems of expressing their thoughts. With practice and experiences of various types, children may acquire an automaticity that will enable them to produce a final product that will meet the standards of good reporting.

Very young children draw pictures to which they give labels. Later, they label their own pictures; then they want complete sentences. At each step, they depend upon someone more capable to record their thoughts. When they have mastered handwriting skills, they can copy what others wrote as they dictated; soon, they can write for themselves. There will be a period of time for the gifted and creative children when they will have thinking and oral language abilities far ahead of their written language skills. Teachers must ensure that such children will have the help needed to record their ideas. If these children are given access to computers, recording ideas will be fun; spelling errors can be corrected later, after the ideas have been recorded and as part of a spelling or proofreading lesson; and fatigue from gripping a pencil will be eliminated. Computers allow children to make changes, deletions, and corrections rather easily and quickly; thus giving them more time and energy to focus on the most important, and often the most frustrating, part of writing—getting one's ideas "down on paper."

If teachers can view creative writing in much the same way that they view drawings or constructions, they will realize that children need freedom to express themselves without fear of criticism, no matter what form of expression is used. At the same time, as teachers provide instruction in basic skills, they will note both progress and problems, resulting in rewards for successes and renewed efforts to master skills.

For children to be able to write creatively, they must be able to think creatively. Programming computers is one way gifted children can develop their creative thinking skills. Teachers should encourage gifted students to learn basic computer programming and to use educational software that strengthens creative thinking skills. When children can think creatively they can also read creatively.

SUMMARY

The goal of reading instruction must extend beyond the mere acquisition of the skill of reading. The ultimate goal must be involvement in the process of reading which results in creative reading and writing. To the extent that we aid children in going beyond merely learning how to read, we are fulfilling our roles as creative teachers.

PART TWO
SPECIAL CONSIDERATIONS

Breaking down barriers to fostering creative reading requires *clarification of problems* and *recommendations for meeting needs.* This section deals with special aspects that must be considered when developing reading programs for gifted and creative learners.

As education moves more and more toward individualization, teachers and parents must seek additional ways to meet individual needs, to innovate, to teach creatively, and to provide for all levels of learners. A vast amount of theoretically sound current information has been presented. The content is valuable to parents and teachers concerned with fostering creative reading at all levels.

The comments concerning home and parent involvement should enable teachers to consider realistically the reasons why some parents have not assumed an adequate role early in their children's lives. Moreover, the ideas presented should motivate teachers to involve parents of older children, as well. Principals and teachers are provided guidance for developing programs for talented learners of all ages in all stages of their thinking and reading growth.

ML

PARENT ROLES IN FOSTERING READING

Edith H. Grotberg
The American University

Parents are particularly important in the development of their gifted and creative children, and the need for schools to work with these parents is increasingly clear. Studies repeatedly show that parents play an active role in the development of their children at home, as they interact with the school in a variety of relationships, and as they help their children develop their gifts and talents on a continuing basis.

THE HOMES OF GIFTED AND CREATIVE CHILDREN

One method for determining what factors are critical to the development of gifted and creative children is to study the homes of both gifted and nongifted children to isolate those things that differentiate the homes. What is present in the homes of the gifted that is absent in the homes of the nongifted? What do parents of the gifted do that parents of the nongifted do not? What is the effect of socioeconomic level? Some of the most important research directed to answering these questions has been done by Ira Gordon and Robert Hess. Further significant studies have been conducted in other countries.

Gordon (4), in his own research and in reviewing the research of others, identified a total of nineteen factors in parent behavior which are related to child performance. Not only is the presence of these factors important to child performance, but of importance also are the degrees to which these factors operate. Of the nineteen critical factors, nine are cognitive or intellectual and ten are emotional or affective. The cognitive factors are as follows:

1. *Academic guidance.* The parents interest their children in learning and exploring activities and encourage them to ask ques-

tions and seek answers. They encourage their children to take initiative and praise them for their efforts.
2. *Cognitive operational level and style.* The parents encourage their children to reason and solve problems and test their ideas with actions. The parents use this cognitive style themselves and provide a model of approach and style.
3. *Cultural activities planned.* The parents expose their children to a large variety of cultural activities. "Let's go to the zoo." "Let's attend the children's concert." "Let's watch this television show." These are some of the planning strategies.
4. *Direct instruction of the child.* The parents teach their children how to do a task, how to solve a problem, how to make choices, and how to assess results. In addition, the parents observe their children as they are learning and offer appropriate suggestions and encouragements.
5. *Educational aspirations.* The parents place high value on education and either actively encourage their children to participate in educational activities and goals or simply assume the children will place value on education because they themselves do. This is generally a valid assumption.
6. *Use of external resources.* The parents have their children attend nursery school or kindergarten or they may place them in special summer activity programs, such as day camp. Many children learn to love books not only because their parents tend to love books, but also because their parents have encouraged them to participate in "the children's hour" at the library.
7. *Intellectuality of the homes.* The parents have books and magazines around the home and usually have dictionaries and encyclopedias. Children see their parents reading these books, using them as references, and discussing what they have read.
8. *Verbal facility.* The parents use words effectively to help their children learn. They do not need large or elaborate vocabularies but they do need to clarify expectations and guide progress verbally.
9. *Verbal frequency.* The parents talk to their children during mealtime, on car trips, and at family gatherings. They use more words than nonverbal signals.

Children need not only cognitive stimulation from their parents but also emotional support if their gifts and talents are to reach fruition. Gor-

don identified the following ten emotional factors in parent behavior which are related to child performance:
1. *Consistency of management.* The parents maintain a consistent and, therefore, predictable style of management or discipline so that the children know what is expected of them and what their limits are. There are no surprises or uncertainties.
2. *Differentiation of self.* The parents do not confuse themselves with their children. They know where their personalities end and and another's begins.
3. *Disciplinary pattern.* The parents behave in their own lives with a sense of self-discipline and an expression of this in their daily performance. The children accept patterns of behavior expressive of this discipline and imitate the models.
4. *Emotional security, self-esteem.* The parents feel safe and loved and respect themselves as significant individuals. They thus have emotional energy available to provide emotional security to their children and opportunities for the children to develop self-esteem.
5. *Impulsivity.* The parents do not engage in erratic, unpredictable behavior, but rather have their behavior under some rational control without repressing creative thoughts and feelings.
6. *Belief in internal control.* The parents stress the importance of building internal controls rather than relying on external controls. Closely allied to this is the belief in assuming responsibility for their own behavior.
7. *Protectiveness, babying of child.* The parents recognize the dependency of their children and are willing to permit them to act out that dependency. The parents provide the protective, nurturing behavior necessary for children to feel protected.
8. *Trusting attitude.* The parents trust each other and trust their children. They encourage their children to trust others and to be receptive to learning experiences might provide. Children who distrust others learn in a distorted way.
9. *Willingness to devote time to the children.* The parents plan activities for their children and enjoy spending time carrying out these activities. Parents need to communicate their pleasure in spending time with their children.
10. *Work habits.* The parents demonstrate to their children that they have developed work habits which permit the acceptance and completion of an activity. The parents also place value on a high level of performance and quality work. They, in effect, respect what they do.

Hess (9) identified nine categories of parent behavior which influence child development: 1) independence training, 2) warmth and high emotional involvement, 3) consistency of discipline, 4) explanatory control, 5) expectation for success, 6) parents' sense of control, 7) the verbalness in the home, 8) parents' direct teaching, and 9) parental self-esteem.

A number of studies of infants also support the contention that parents influence the development of their children. The Illinois study (21) found several items which consistently related to child cognitive performance in the first two years of life: "There was at least one magazine placed where the child could play with it or look at it; the child was given regular training in one or more skills; the mother spontaneously vocalized to the child; the mother spontaneously named at least one object to the child while the observer was in the home; the father helped take care of the child; the father played with the child at least ten minutes a day; the child was regularly spoken to by parents during mealtimes."

Miller (16), in reviewing the research on the relationships between family variables and scholastic performance in English schools, lists the following as positively related to school performance: "homes where independent thinking and freedom of discussion occur, where there are values conducive to intellectual effort, where children's curiosity and academic aspirations are supported, and in which there is harmony between home and school values."

Keeves (13), in an extensive study of early adolescents in the Australian capitol territory, uncovered relationships between school performance and home environment. He reported that "...the importance of the mother's attitudes and ambitions stands out quite clearly, but are exceeded in importance by the provision made in the home for stimulation to learn and to promote intellectual development."

In a study in Utrecht, Holland, Rupp (11) indicated the "cultural-pedagogical aspects of upbringing" and found that, when high achievers were compared with low achievers within the lowest socioeconomic class, the high achievers came from homes in which parents held this cultural-pedagogical point of view. They saw themselves as educators. They practice this by "reading to their children, playing table games and word games with them, providing educational toys and books, reading and possessing books themselves, telling their children informative things of their own accord, teaching their children preschool skills, going to places of interest."

It is important to note how frequently emotional factors are identified as critical to promoting gifts and talents in children. Not only do parents help their children more when they themselves have a good sense of who they are, a feeling of stabiliy and emotional security, and a sense of control and worth, but they also need to be supportive and encouraging of their children. Patterns of parental indifference, rejection, or oversolicitude impair the children's development and may crush their talents. One expression of this turmoil is underachievement (6, 7).

The assumption that gifted and creative children come only from advantaged homes or higher-income homes is questionable. In earlier studies, from Terman (20) to Martinson (15), gifted and creative children emerge from a cross section of the socioeconomic spectrum.

In a careful review of the research on the effect of socioeconomic level of the home on the development of the child, Gordon (4) found some evidence that middle-income parents tended to have more effective techniques with their children than lower income parents. He cautioned, however, that his research, as well as that of Hess and Shipman (9), White (23), and Watts (22), indicates tremendous variability within social class groups. Gordon states: "If we are interested in identifying particular parental attributes which we feel are desirable, then social class is not a usable label....Our infant research all clearly indicates that the amount of conversation in the home, particularly the *amount* directed toward the child, relates significantly to child performance."

PARENTS AS TEACHERS

Parents provide an environment in which their children are totally immersed. Most early childhood experiences are within a parent-determined environment, but parents are generally unaware that they are performing as teachers. Parents need to be made aware of their role as teachers and then to acquire teaching skills to enhance the development of their children. Research describes how parents, once aware of their role, affect the learning of their children. Teaching includes setting the stage for learning, modeling, managing the environment, giving information, and engaging in direct interaction. These components of teaching are incorporated in numerous research studies. The research findings relate to the effects on children of programs which focus heavily on teaching the child with some parent involvement as teachers.

Virtually all of the recent and current research relating to parents as teachers focuses on low-income parents and their children. Those few studies which include middle-income and mixed socioeconomic groups use these groups mainly for comparison purposes. Almost without exception, the parent involved is the mother. Few fathers have participated in these programs; those who have are apt to have participated either in decision-making positions or in programs designed to increase the skill of the father for his own development.

SPECIAL PROGRAMS

Training Parents as Teachers

Programs which are largely parent-oriented include using television as a medium of instruction, training parents to work in the home with their children, and training parents through group discussion techniques.

In almost all of the studies in which mothers are trained to tutor their children at home, the children show immediate gains in intellectual, conceptual, or language development. These findings occur in projects involving home visits only, in preschool projects operated in the home, in preschool plus home visiting projects, and in projects in which the mothers are trained to work at home with their children but receive few, if any, home visits. Lazar and Chapman (14), report that in four studies parent-teaching with or without a preschool component resulted in greater immediate effect on children's language, intellectual, or academic achievement than a preschool program only. In one project concerned with infants, superiority of the experimental group of children was not maintained at age two if parent-teaching was terminated at age one, but it was maintained if parent teaching continued until the child reached age two.

Though relatively few studies have included a follow up of these home teaching programs, those which did usually reported that gains continued to be apparent. In two projects having only a home visit and introducing parent-teaching after age one, intellectual levels remained significantly high. In two projects involving preschool plus home visits, experimental group children showed beneficial effects upon entering school and through the middle primary grades without further parent-teaching.

The few results available on the impact of parent-teaching in association with educational televison programs suggest that parental encouragement and parent-child activities related to such programs for young children may enhance the cognitive gains made by the children as a result of the television program.

Though difficult, it is possible to engage a sizeable proportion of low-income mothers of preschool children in groups to discuss concerns about themselves, their communities, and their children. A number of studies have reported that the skill and sensitivity of the group leader or trainer is crucial in getting the parents to attend the sessions and to participate actively in the group. While those parents who attend such groups represent a self-selected population, which no doubt differs from the nonattending parents, they do generally express positive feelings about the effect of the group experience on themselves and on the behavior of their children. A number of studies have reported greater success in gaining attendance and participation of mothers when the content of the program was specific, such as language development, rather than sensitivity training or general discussions of child development. Two studies have reported greater immediate gains by the children with mothers in a structural language curriculum, compared to other types of discussion groups. Follow up on most studies has been lacking.

Partial Involvement of Parents as Teachers

These programs focus primarily on the child, while the role of the parent is of secondary or even incidental emphasis. Even among these studies, however, children in a preschool program tend to show greater immediate gains in IQ and achievement when their parents participate in a parent educational component aimed at increasing cognitive development. Other studies report no significant differences among the groups of children but have found some differences in attitude among the mothers. Some studies have reported greater group gains among mothers and children when the mothers have participated in a specific language training program to augment the program of their children, than when mothers take part in other group activities. One study indicates the possibility of "sleeper" effects, in that attitude change among the mothers in the experimental group was not reflected in difference between groups of children until a later follow up. A number of ongoing and completed studies are attempting to bring about changes in mother-child interaction through behavior modification techniques which would supplement the program focusing primarily on the child.

In summary, most of the studies which focused on training mothers as teachers of their children report positive immediate effects as the intellectual achievement or language development of the children. Studies which have provided a parent-teaching component as an adjunct to an ongoing children's program also show positive changes among the children but not with the same frequency as when parents are the primary focus of the training. These studies, however, concern young children and their parents. Very little has been done to study the effects on older children of parent-teaching activities. And yet children should benefit from parent-teaching experiences at any age.

The alert parents, for example, who know their children have learned how to read maps in school may well involve their children in planning family trips. Together, they study the maps to determine route, road conditions, stopping places, and time involved. Parents do not need special training for this kind of activity, but they do need to know the skills their children have acquired and the uses to which they might be applied.

The concerned teachers at grades three, seven, or eleven may send home a book list for suggested birthday or Christmas gifts for children. The teacher may also encourage the children to involve their parents in research projects, particularly those involving reading. The teacher may find the parents so interested that they seek a closer relationship with the teacher in order to enhance the development of gifts and talents in their children.

Teachers may assume that parents who have not expressed an interest in helping their children do not wish to help them. The fact might well be that parents believe they are not to "interfere" with the education of their children, particularly as they move into higher grades. Further, parents who do not perceive their parent-teaching capability may appreciate some guidance from teachers. Teachers surely have an obligation to determine at any grade what the parents might do to help their gifted children. And teachers have the knowledge and skills to show parents how to become involved in the development of their gifted and talented children.

HOME/SCHOOL RELATIONSHIPS

Homes cannot become schools any more than schools can become homes. They have unique functions which need to be maintained and respected. Nor can there be an unrestricted open-door policy. Schools should not tolerate an unannounced invasion by parents any more than homes should tolerate the unannounced home visit by teachers. The two institutions need some clear areas of separate autonomy, but large areas of cooperation remain, and we must address ourselves to these areas if we want our gifted and talented children to fulfill themselves. The interaction between home and school may take place in the home, in the school or preschool, or in a neighborhood learning center. Evidence has already been provided from the research literature that such interactions benefit children, but the research has not exhausted the possibilities for home/school cooperation nor has this research generally addressed older children. The recommendations presented here are partially based on

research evidence but attempt to go beyond that evidence to recommendations based on observation and experience.
1. *Bring the school to the home.* The expertise of the school is in learning-teaching. Materials, curricula, and a vast array of ideas and skills address the learning-teaching phenomenon. The school may bring these materials, ideas, and skills into the home through a home visitor, a resource teacher, or a mobile unit. School personnel may demonstrate activities in the home, leave materials on a lend-lease basis, or leave materials appropriate for a television show. The parents may ask questions, report progress, and indeed demonstrate their skills with their children.

As children advance in school, they themselves can bring home materials and activities to elicit from their parents insights and assistance. Homework generally seems to separate students from parents rather than encouraging students to benefit from their parents' knowledge. Older children might bring home materials for their younger brothers and sisters and enjoy the experience of teaching them, reading to them, or engaging in some learning activity with them.

2. *Bring the home to the school.* Parents should be able to use many school facilities to help their children.
    a. Use the library. Schools need to include library materials for parents who wish to read books for deeper understanding of their children, to read to their children, or to learn how to do things with their children. The International Reading Association published a helpful guide, *Reading for the Gifted and the Creative Student,* edited by Paul Witty.
    b. Have their children screened. Many promising children are handicapped by perceptual problems and learning difficulties. Just as medical doctors screen for health problems and dentists for dental problems, teachers should provide preschool as well as in-school screening to identify learning problems.

        Screening for talent is another important service the school can (and indeed, some schools do) provide. Talents and gifts need nurturing from early childhood and many parents either do not recognize the gifts of their children or do not know what they can do to help their children. In conjunction with early screening services, schools can guide parents in readings and activities to enhance the talents of their children.

    c. Observe classroom activities. Parents who watch their children in a classroom are able to learn how to enhance children's learning. Indeed, with some guidance from teachers, parents may supplement and reinforce classroom activities and learning experiences, thus preventing a dichotomy between home and school.
    d. Attend cultural activities. The school needs to be a cultural center for families. When children perform in plays, play an instrument in the orchestra, or have an art exhibit, both they and their parents may share a cultural activity. Some schools involve parents in organizing and planning for cultural activities.
3. *Establish community learning centers.* As an alternative to the home or the school being the locus for home/school cooperation, a community learning center has been suggested. This concept emerges from the increased awareness that the whole child, and not just cognitive development, must be the focus of our attention if the child is to develop fully. A community learning center might have materials on health and physical well-being; it might have a pediatrician, a psychologist, and an educator. Parents would bring their children to the center for diagnosis and screening to identify problems and to determine gifts and talents. The same center might provide materials, books, and guidance to parents. The entire family could attend activities together in the evening or on weekends and extend the children's learning experiences to the larger social community.

    Many of these recommendations are in operation or are in the process of being implemented. All of the services must, of course, be used at the option of the parents.

    But there seems little risk that such services will not be used. Parents have become extremely sensitive to their role in enhancing the development of their children, to the need for early identification and stimulation of gifts and talents, and to the need to look to schools and other community resources. The school may lag behind parents in these understandings and may need some prodding from the parents. For the sake of the gifts and talents of their children, let them prod.

SUMMARY

    As children's first educators, parents are the first to be in a position to recognize unusual or remarkable abilities in their children. Research documents the effects of parent involvement and interaction with their children. Children are clearly helped or hindered in their development by the nature and quality of parent involvement. The importance of engaging in activities together, of talking together, of reading together—and for children to hear their parents read to them—is stressed over and over. Teachers do not generally become involved with the education of children until after much learning has already occurred. It is important, then, for teachers to coordinate their efforts with what parents have already accomplished and to perceive the school/home environment relationship as a cooperative venture for the benefit of the development of children. This cooperation may begin at any time during the school years if early efforts were overlooked.

References
1. Alvino, James. "How to Nurture Children's Creativity and Critical Thinking Skills," *PTA Today,* 9 (November 1983), 13-16. (EJ288980 SP513388)
2. Baskin, Barbara H., and Karen H. Harris. *Books for the Gifted Child.* New York: R.R. Bowker, 1980.
3. Ehrlich, Virginia Z. *Gifted Children: A Guide for Parents and Teachers.* Englewood Cliffs, New Jersey: Prentice-Hall. 1982.
4. Gordon, I.R. *Parent Involvement in Compensatory Education.* Urbana, Illinois: University of Illinois Press, 1970.
5. Gordon, I.R. "What Do We Know About Parents-as-Teachers?" Paper presented at the American Educational Research Association Convention, 1972.
6. Gowan, John C. "The Underachieving Gifted Child: A Problem for Everyone," *Exceptional Children,* 21 (April 1955), 247-249.
7. Grotberg, Edith H. "Adjustment Problems of the Gifted," *Education,* 82 (April 1962), 474-476.
8. Hall, Eleanor G., and Nancy Skinner. *Somewhere to Turn: Strategies for Parents of the Gifted and Talented.* New York: Teachers College Press, Columbia University, 1980.
9. Hess, R.D., and V. Shipman. "Cognitive Elements in Maternal Behavior," in J.P. Hill (Ed.), *Minnesota Symposia on Child Psychology,* Volume I. Minneapolis: University of Minnesota Press, 1967.
10. Hess, R.D. "Community Involvement in Day Care," in Edith H. Grotberg (Ed.), *Day Care: Resources for Decisions.* Office of Economic Opportunity, 1971.
11. Johnson, Lynn G. "A Better Time for Development than Identification," *Roeper Review,* 5 (April-May 1983), 13-15. (EJ 282773 EC 152329)
12. Karnes, Frances A., and Emily C. Collins. *Handbook of Instructional Resources and References for Teaching the Gifted.* Boston: Allyn & Bacon, 1980.
13. Keeves, J.P. "The Home Environment and Educational Achievement," unpublished manuscript, Australian-National University, 1970.

14. Lazar, Joyce B., and Judith Chapman. *A Review of the Present Status and Future Research Needs of Programs to Develop Parenting Skills,* prepared for the Interagency Panel on Early Childhood Research and Development. Washington, D.C.: George Washington University, 1972.
15. Martinson, Ruth. *Educational Programs for Gifted Pupils.* Sacramento: California State Department of Education, 1961.
16. Miller, G.W. *Educational Opportunity and the Home.* London: Longman, 1971.
17. Passow, A. Harry (Ed.). *The Gifted and the Talented: Their Educational Development,* The Seventy-Eight Yearbook of the National Society for the Study of Education. Chicago: University of Chicago Press, 1979.
18. Rupp, J.C.C. *Helping the Child to Cope With School.* Groninger, Netherlands: Wolters-Noodhott, 1969.
19. Sieglebaum, Laura, and Susan Rotner. "Ideas and Activities for Parents of Preschool Gifted Children," *Gifted Child Quarterly,* 26 (January-February 1983), 40-44. (EJ 278105 EC 151844)
20. Terman, L.M. *Genetic Studies of Genius.* Stanford, California: Stanford University Press, 1925-1959.
21. Wachs, T.D., I.C. Uzgiris, and J. McV. Hunt. "Cognitive Development in Infants of Different Age Levels and from Different Environmental Backgrounds: An Exploratory Investigation," *Merrill-Palmer Quarterly,* 17 (1971), 283-317.
22. Watts, J.C., and J.C. Barnett. "Environment," mimeo manuscript, 1971.
23. White, B.L. "Fundamental Early Environmental Influences on the Development of Competency," in M. Meyer (Ed.), *Third Symposium on Learning: Cognitive Learning.* Bellingham, Washington: Western Washington State College, 1972.

LANGUAGE PROGRAMS FOR YOUNG CHILDREN: IMPLICATIONS FOR THE CREATIVE AND GIFTED

Dorothy S. Strickland
Teachers College
Columbia University

The kind of education which a child receives in an early childhood program is largely determined by the philosophy of those who develop that program. This philosophy helps shape the curriculum, sets the tone for the overall learning environment, and ultimately determines the type of materials available to the child.

CURRENT PHILOSOPHICAL VIEWS

One of the major current philosophical conflicts facing early childhood educators today is focused on preschool or pre-first grade experience. This conflict holds far reaching implications for the creative and gifted child. Elkind (1) sees it as a "battle between the traditional middle-class nursery school teachers who see preschool education as development from within and the new breed of preschool workers who see education as enforcement from without." In its extreme form, the conflict exists between those who hold that the purpose of preschool education is to enrich the life of the young child through a program entirely focused on social development and their opponents who place major emphasis on the direct instruction of specific skills and behaviors they consider important for success in school.

DETERMINING GOALS

Of course, few programs actually reflect such extremes in philosophy. Out of this very conflict, however, come a number of basic issues which early childhood teachers face as they plan for the children in their charge. On the one hand, most teachers would agree that socialization and self-expression should receive heavy emphasis in their programs. They recognize that readiness is a phenomenon which is determined primarily by each individual child's own rate of development; therefore, they would avoid academic pressure. At the same time, these teachers are faced with the equally important need to provide challenging cognitive experiences which will allow young children varied opportunities to acquire information and skills. The problem of providing academic stimulation without academic pressure lies at the heart of curriculum planning for all children in early childhood settings. Planning for gifted and creative children, however, requires special care to set goals which demand a balance between academic stimulation and social, emotional and physical needs.

When planning language and literacy related experiences at this level, early childhood teachers are faced with many decisions. They must decide how much, if any, time to give to direct instruction of a set of specific skills. If they do give direct instruction they must decide what content to include and what method of classroom organization will be most helpful. Thus, teachers must resolve the question of what combination of whole-group instruction, small-group instruction, and individualized instruction to use. If no direct instruction is to be given, the question is whether reliance on incidental learning and self discovery will be sufficient to meet the goals of the program.

Teachers must decide how to view cognitive development—in terms of the content mastered or in terms of the process involved? For reading, this may mean the difference between a program that heavily emphasizes the recognition of letters and words as opposed to a program that places as much or more importance on affective learnings such as creative drama and the enjoyment of literature.

Another important question is whether the early childhood teacher's primary responsibility is that of preparation for the future or planning for present needs. Whether to focus language arts experiences toward a goal of getting the children ready for some future grade or level, or to base those experiences on the assessment of the current needs and interests of the children for use as an avenue for language growth is another critical decision.

PROGRAM PLANNING

The kinds of materials found in an early childhood classroom will reflect the way the person responsible for the program has answered the questions raised above. In the interest of all children but especially the gifted and creative, let us hope that the teacher faced with these choices will decide in favor of a total language arts program with clearly defined goals which relate primarily to individuals rather than to the group.

In addition, although most programs include varying amounts of direct instruction, undirected learning through a wide variety of materials should also be heavily relied upon. Broad goals should be set for the entire group, but major attention should be given to setting goals and expectations which are deliberately different for each child. The materials in such a program would necessarily provide for a wide range of abilities and capabilities.

Cognitive development should be viewed in terms of process rather than product, allowing for a broad range of activities rather than a narrow program designed to promote a set of specific skills. The use of drama, music, art, and movement would become a significant part of the language arts program. The process of making one's own materials would be an extremely important experience for the child. Thus, commercially prepared materials, teacher-made materials, and materials prepared by the students would all receive status in the program.

Let us also hope that these teachers will decide against a language program which focuses entirely on getting children ready for some future grade or level. When future accomplishment is the main concern of the language arts program, the reading curriculum tends to be relatively fixed and little flexibility is allowed for individual differences. Planning for present needs allows for a wide range of learning opportunities which enable children to progress as rapidly as their interests and abilities will allow.

There should be an adequate, continual assessment of abilities for all children. For gifted and creative children, there would then be an early identification of talent and superior potential. Early identification is important for both the child who learns to read before formal instruction normally begins and for the child who does not learn to read early but who needs to be encouraged to move ahead to more advanced work as soon as the need or desire is expressed.

The program would set no minimum standards of achievement for all children, since such standards generally become the norm for the entire group and therefore may be too optimistic for the slow child and too limiting for the gifted child. The materials in such a program would provide for the broad range of differences within the group. It is quite possible and desirable that everything, from blocks and beads to easy readers and dictionaries, would be found in the same classroom. Moreover, all children may use the entire range of materials as needs arise.

Research suggests that providing a generally enriched environment should be the guiding principle for planning early childhood programs. Enrichment by providing more depth or breadth in the curriculum and stimulating higher level thinking processes can benefit both gifted and nongifted children (2). At the preschool and primary grade levels, nongifted children usually show a lack of interest in activities beyond their level (3). An enriched program offers the benefits of exposure to more challenging learning opportunities for all children, as it fills the particular requirements for those who may be gifted (4).

SELECTING MATERIALS

When considering materials, the teacher's first responsibility is to insure a stimulating room environment. Just as the housekeeping corner, the block area, and the art center are valuable in an early childhood program, a language arts center should also be part of that program. This area would be a place where children go to read and write.

For reading, the center should be equipped with picture books, picture story books, easy readers, and books made by the teacher and by the children. Experience charts and stories should be hung on the walls or on easels. A list of the children's names, magazines, puzzles, and language games should all be available.

For writing, sufficient pencils, crayons, magic markers, and other types of writing materials should be available. Plenty of paper in all sizes, shapes, and colors should be ready and waiting. The center should also have a primary typewriter for typing one's name or a note or a list or just for the fun of finding the letters one knows.

The literature collection in such a classroom should be both broad and varied. It will go beyond the usual collection of ABC, counting, nursery rhyme, poetry, nature, and story books to include a large assortment of easy reading material. Heavy emphasis should be placed on concept books dealing with a variety of abstract ideas. Catalogs and old magazines should be on hand for use as picture resources or for browsing. Children's magazines and reference materials should be available. Gifted and creative children are especially curious during these early years and require many resources for the answers to their constant questions; teachers can expect gifted and creative children to use dictionaries, encyclopedias, and other resource materials frequently, perhaps with the help of the teacher, other adults, and older children.

A collection of pictures, classified and filed according to subject and/ or use, can be an invaluable aid to the early childhood teacher. Such pictures may be used as stimulators for discussion, storytelling, role playing, and vocabulary building activities. Small pictures may be used for classification exercises.

An assortment of audiovisual materials should also be included in a well-equipped early childhood classroom. A record player for listening to stories, music, and poetry is important. A tape recorder will provide endless hours of enjoyable and purposeful activity. Children especially enjoy reading original stories based on textless picture storybooks. A puppet theater and puppets may be used for creative dramatics. A flannel board may be used in a number of ways, including classifying information and retelling stories while putting cutouts in proper sequence.

SUMMARY

The early years require a flexible program for children if they are to be guided toward maximum achievement and the expression of talent. An early childhood program that recognizes this will be staffed with teachers who, because they are knowledgeable about the characteristics of young gifted and creative students, will insure their early identification. Such a program will support and motivate these children, allowing them to progress as fast and as far as their interests and abilities will allow. The language arts curriculum will provide a broad range of experiences for all children so that those who exhibit early reading potential may receive the freedom to learn to read with complete support and encouragement. Most important, the language arts program will provide abundant opportunities for all children to participate in a variety of intellectually stimulating activities. This is essential if young children are to develop their full potential for successful learning.

References
1. Elkind, David. "Preschool Education: Enrichment or Instruction?" *Childhood Education,* 45 (February 1969), 321-328.
2. Kitano, Margie. "Young Gifted Children: Strategies for Preschool Teachers," *Young Children,* 37 (May 1982), 14-24.
3. Malone, C.E. "Early Childhood Education of Gifted Children," *Gifted Child Quarterly,* 18 (1974), 188-190.
4. Strickland, Dorothy. "Nurturing Gifts and Talents of Young Learners," In W.L. Marks and R.O. Nystrand (Eds.), *Strategies for Educational Change: Recognizing the Gifts and Talents of All Children.* New York: Macmillan, 1983, 181-192.

USING READING TO STIMULATE CREATIVE THINKING IN THE INTERMEDIATE GRADES

Richard J. Smith
University of Wisconsin at Madison

In *The Prophet,* Gibran (3) writes that if a teacher "...is indeed wise, he does not bid you enter the house of his wisdom, but rather leads you to the threshold of your own mind." As a vehicle for taking students to the thresholds of their own minds, reading has few equals. Torrance (11) says, "A good story, biography, or other reading material is likely to evoke many ideas and questions which can send the reader far beyond what is read." Students who do not develop the habit of reading beyond the lines miss the many pleasant intellectual excursions they might take while reading.

Consider the following passage from *The Comeback Guy* (2): "Once more he visualized himself standing, pole poised, at the end of the runway. Down the runway, high in the sky above the pit, the crossbar swayed gently, challenging him and mocking him." The student who pauses to see, in her mind's eye, Jeff's vaulting over the bar or twisting his ankle, and to hear the words of praise or sighs of disappointment from Jeff's schoolmates, has taken advantage of some of the thinking potential in the story. Another student reading the same passage might pause briefly to recall the time he himself stood at home plate with two strikes and the winning run on third. He might form in his mind the words, "Do it, Jeff," as he supplies the colors, the sounds, and the smells the author didn't describe when he wrote the story. Readers who make these kinds of additions to the material they read are creative readers.

Creative reading is an elusive concept, and different people who write about the phenomenon may conceptualize it differently. Perhaps Johnson (4) comes close to the conceptualization offered here when he says, "Reading is something we do, not so much with our eyes, as such, as with our knowledge and interests and enthusiasm, our hatred and fondnesses and fears, our evaluations in all their forms and aspects." The teacher's job is to teach this concept to students and to give them opportunities to express the ideas and feelings that are born as what they have learned in the past combines with the ideas and feelings they experience as they are reading.

Teachers have been concerned about "individualizing" reading instruction ever since the fact of individual differences in learning was accepted by the educational community. Creative reading is a highly individual process. Letting each student supply personal additions to a particular selection is certainly one dimension of individualizing instruction. Thirty students responding differently to the same story, poem, or newspaper article can be just as much of an individualized reading activity as thirty students responding to thirty different selections. Obviously, students must be taught to learn what the author put on the page before they create additions of their own. But when students have been encouraged to add something to their material as they have read, teachers must be prepared to accept their creations as expressions of individuality and not expect the work of one student to resemble the work of another student or look like the product the teacher would have created, given the same task.

READING AS THINKING

Creative reading is difficult to define because the nature of the phenomenon is highly individual and complex. Perhaps creative reading can be best conceptualized as a level or kind of thinking behavior. If Bloom's *Taxonomy of Educational Objectives* (1) is used as a reference to specify a particular cognitive level for creative thinking, then the level of "synthesis" seems to provide the best fit. At this level, thinking is the process of working with elements or parts and combining them in such a way as to constitute a pattern or structure not clearly there before. This requires a recombination of parts or all of a previous experience with new material, reconstructed into a new and integrated whole. Applied to reading, this means that ideas acquired from a reading selection are combined with ideas or information acquired elsewhere in a purposeful search for a new product, pattern, or structure (e.g., additional dialogue, an original drawing, a puppet show, a different story ending, a new character).

The images, dialogue, sounds, speculations, and other creations arising in the mind of a reader as spin-offs from an author's words can do much to enhance the understanding and enjoyment of selections that lend themselves to creative thinking. One of the characteristics of reluctant readers, or readers with poorly developed basic reading skills, is that they don't add anything to the material they read. Consequently, they miss the exhilaration that comes from investing something of oneself in a story, poem, or exposition. Otto and Smith (7) say, "The student who brings the full range of his thinking and feeling powers to a reading act is a mature reader. He comprehends not only the stated but also the implied meanings of the author...as he reads, he learns, applies, analyzes, synthesizes, and evaluates. He is satisfied, frustrated, delighted, disquieted."

SPECIAL CHARACTERISTICS OF INTERMEDIATE GRADE CHILDREN

The fostering of creative thinking relative to reading selections is possible and desirable at all academic levels for students who have mastered the basic decoding and comprehension skills. During intermediate grades students appear to have both the maturity and the basic abilities to benefit greatly from well-designed programs.

Torrance (12) says, "Children between ten and twelve delight in exploration, girls preferring to explore in books and in pretend play and boys through first-hand experiences. It is a great age for reading. They have now become less restless and can read or think for long periods....The child at this stage...is capable of deriving principles or generalizations or devising schemes to express sympathy, if challenged to do so. He seldom does so on his own initiative." Smith and Barrett (19) say,

> Although reading may be used to foster creative behavior at all academic levels, the intermediate grades are particularly well suited to this kind of activity. Students in the intermediate grades have a greater wealth of background experiences than primary grade students and are not so inhibited in regard to divergent thinking as older students often become. Both of these characteristics are important to the success of reading-related activities designed to foster creativity. To be creative the student must draw upon his repertoire of experiences and arrange them in a pattern that is different from any previous pattern in his thinking. To do this he must "dare to be different." The playful, yet purposeful, behavior inherent in creativity lends itself well to the mind of the preadolescent.

The emerging importance of the content area curriculums is another factor that causes the intermediate grades to be fertile ground for developing the habit of thinking creatively while reading. After grade three, reading materials in the content areas rapidly become more sophisticated in both information and linguistic structure. Questions and tasks that encourage students to combine new information with experiences they have had in other contexts for the creation of some product they can share with interested people can make the reading of content more productive in terms of both enjoyment and information gained.

PROCEDURES THAT ENCOURAGE CREATIVE READING

Undoubtedly, some students learn to respond creatively to reading selections without formal instruction. However, the large number of students at all academic levels who seem unable to respond to a reading selection with more than short answers to factual questions suggests the need for formal instruction in this important dimension of the reading program. Perhaps a major problem is that many reading materials and coordinated instructional activities seem to work against the development of thinking creatively while reading. Too heavy reliance upon workbooks, kits, and other developmental reading materials in the instructional program may cause students to perceive reading as no more than a matter of superficially reading a short selection (which is often of questionable literary quality) and answering five or ten multiple-choice questions. Many times the questions are constructed to allow students to evaluate their reading ability by checking their answers against an answer key, thereby eliminating questions requiring more than a direct statement or several words as an answer. Certainly, these materials give little encouragement to add something to the selection from the students' personal experiences.

Reading Literature

The key to fostering the habit of reading creatively, then, may lie in 1) finding material with interesting characters and situations, vivid descriptions, well-chosen words, and other features that permit students to empathize, visualize, and think through an idea with an author; and 2) structuring reading-related instructional activities that give students direction and parameters without focusing their thinking so sharply that the process of synthesizing information is stifled or the emergence of personal feelings is repressed.

In *Raccoons Are the Brightest People,* North (5) writes, "Pet deer clearly marked with red ribbons and with antlers stained with Mercurochrome are murdered almost every year by poachers, usually as the trusting animal walks to within ten or fifteen feet of these 'licensed murderers' invading posted land." Teachers might ask students individually, in pairs, or in small groups to use this passage as a point of departure for the following activities:

1. Writing a dialogue between a game warden and a poacher who has just killed a deer illegally.
2. Producing a mock court trial for a man accused of killing an animal out of season.
3. Planning a scene for a movie or a TV drama in which a poacher kills someone's pet. (Lighting, background music, costumes, close-up shots, setting, and other elements could be taken into consideration.)
4. Writing a letter to the editor from a farmer whose cow was killed by a deer hunter.
5. Creating a lecture that Sterling North might give the members of the National Rifle Association at their annual convention.

These creative activities are fun and they help students develop their language skills. But they also train students to engage in creative thinking while they read. How many readers have been disappointed by movie versions because in their creative reading they had imagined characters and settings differently from the way Hollywood interpreted them?

Good questions get students' imaginations working. They stimulate thinking as the creative readers process the words and sentences that in one sense are the same for everyone who reads them and in another sense different for everyone who reads them.

Smith (8) has prepared guidelines for the construction of questions and tasks designed to stimulate students to think creatively as they read: 1) They ask for information that is not in the material; 2) they ask for the reader's personal ideas; 3) they do not attempt to evoke responses that can be judged as correct or incorrect, and 4) they focus on what the reader can add to the material. Intermediate grade students can learn quickly to recognize questions that send them on a thoughtful, purposeful mental trip beyond the boundaries of the story into unfamiliar territory.

In *The Light in the Forest,* Richter (7) writes, "The two marched on in silence. When they came to the river's edge, Half Arrow stepped aside and True Son waded in alone....Not until he was out and dripping on the other side and following the trail on the bank with the column did he look back. Far across the water he could make out two figures. They were Half Arrow and Little Crane, standing at the water's edge. Their eyes he knew strained after him. He wished he could hold up his hand in farewell, but his arms were tied. Then he passed with his companions into the forest."

This is the final paragraph in Chapter Four and a good point of departure for some creative thinking activities. Students at this point in the novel might be asked to do one or more of the following:

1. Imagine Half Arrow and Little Crane returning to their camp. What are their thoughts? What words pass between them? Describe the scene around the Indian campfire that night.
2. If Half Arrow were to make a speech to his tribe that night, what would he say?
3. Write an entry for Little Crane's diary in which he describes the day's events, his feelings, and his speculations about the future.

Writing in the first person, Taylor (*10*) in *The Cay* creates the character of a young man cast away on a lonely Caribbean island with an old Black West Indian sailor. Reading about the relationship which grows between the young man and the old sailor—in part because of an injury that blinds the young man—is highly revealing of human nature to many students in the intermediate grades. The story ends with the following passage: "Maybe I won't know it by sight, but when I go ashore and close my eyes, I'll know this was our own cay. I'll walk along east beach and out to the reef. I'll go up the hill to the row of palm trees and stand by his grove." Students enjoy role playing, and this story provides many opportunities for them—perhaps to create a new character who joins the two castaways at some point in the narrative or to plan and present a "Meet the Press" program in which the young man is interviewed by members of the press about his adventures.

Reading in the Content Areas

At some time during the intermediate grades students usually study ecology in science. The reading materials might lead to the creation of letters to the editor regarding pollution control, mock trials of industries accused of polluting rivers with their wastes, or a list of rules for campers to follow—ranging from having their automobiles well tuned to the use of minibikes on forest trails. One science teacher had the animals of the forest sue campers for the anguish and physical damage they had suffered. His seventh graders set up a trial situation with one student representing the deer, another the fish, and others in special roles. The students had to do considerable "noncreative" as well as creative reading for this project.

Language arts teachers might ask students to read a story as a television or movie producer would read it in adapting it for another medium. Students would identify scenes that would be highlighted or cut, desirable settings, actors for the leading roles, and other aspects that must be considered in television and movie production. Poems often suggest visual images or feelings that can be represented by combinations of colors or abstract drawings. Stanzas can be added to poems and new endings can be supplied for short stories.

Physical education teachers can assign students to read the sports pages in their daily newspapers and write "guess who" dialogues between a quarterback and his coach concerning some performance during the game of the week. Students can be asked to write about a game as a biographer might write about it in "The Story of Johnny Unitas" or "Bobby Hull in Action." Or students can compose a letter that Babe Ruth might have written to Henry Aaron as Aaron broke Ruth's home run record. Boxing fans can supply the words that Joe Frazier and Muhammad Ali might have exchanged in a particular round.

When social studies teachers have ascertained that their students understand what the author of their history text has written about the signing of the Declaration of Independence, the teachers can ask students to engage in one or more of the following activities:

1. You have read that Adams and Franklin made some changes in Jefferson's draft of the Declaration. Pretend that the three of them have met to discuss those changes. Who would begin the conversation? How would Jefferson react to the knowledge that someone had changed what he had written with such emotion and dedication? How might the history of this nation have been changed by the meeting?
2. Imagine that you are a group of colonists in the park reading the Declaration for the first time. How do you feel? What do you say? Do some role playing in small groups.
3. You are a colonist with some artistic talent and you know this Declaration means war and that soldiers will have to be recruited for an army. Design a poster urging able-bodied colonists to enlist in the new colonial army.
4. Write a letter that Benjamin Franklin might have written to a good friend of his in London or Paris shortly after he signed the Declaration. Remember, he's an old man with much experience and many accomplishments behind him.

GUIDELINES FOR CREATIVE READING INSTRUCTION

The possibilities for training students to let their minds travel some of the side roads as well as the main highways while reading are limited only by the imagination of teachers and their willingness to construct questions and activities that introduce students to the many possibilities for divergent thinking that present themselves in reading selections. Teachers should be aware of certain conditions that must be present to attain the objectives of creative reading.

1. The material must be suitable for creative thinking. Tasks that are strained to fit unsuitable material usually result in strained or illogical responses.
2. Students need time for the synthesizing process to work. Creativity cannot be rushed.
3. Students and teachers must learn that products resulting from creative thinking relative to reading selections cannot be graded or evaluated as correct or incorrect.
4. The assigned questions and tasks must be reasonable expectations for the students who receive them. Few, if any, students in the intermediate grades can redesign a skyscraper or write an original musical score for *Tarzan and the Jewels of Opar.*

SUMMARY

A reading selection, a carefully constructed task to stimulate creative thinking about that selection, and the mind of a student in the intermediate grades can become a powerful combination for generating an original idea or product. Important also to the process of creation is an environment that encourages a searching mind and provides time to let that mind synthesize information and feelings arising from a variety of experiences. Teachers must provide all of the conditions that foster creativity if students are to use reading as a springboard to a new idea, feeling, or tangible product.

Learning to think creatively while one reads is like most other learned behaviors. Students need instruction, practice, and positive reinforcement for their efforts. They especially need teachers who believe that the fostering of creative thinking relative to a reading selection is an important objective of the reading curriculum.

References
1. Bloom, Benjamin et al. *Taxonomy of Educational Objectives.* New York: McKay, 1956.
2. Frick, C. H. *The Comeback Guy.* New York: Harcourt Brace Jovanovich, 1961, 76.
3. Gibran, Kahlil. "On Teaching," *The Prophet.* New York: Alfred A. Knopf, 1965, 56.

4. Johnson, Wendell. *Your Most Enchanted Listener.* New York: Harper and Row, 1956, 123.
5. North, Sterling. *Raccoons Are the Brightest People.* New York: Avon Books, 1966, 157.
6. Otto, Wayne, and Richard J. Smith. *Administering the School Reading Program.* Boston: Houghton Mifflin, 1970, 72.
7. Richter, Conrad. *The Light in the Forest.* New York: Bantam Books, 1953, 22.
8. Smith, Richard J. "Questions for Teachers—Creative Reading," *The Reading Teacher,* February 1969, 430-434, 439.
9. Smith, Richard J., and Thomas C. Barrett. *Teaching Reading in the Middle Grades.* Reading, Massachusetts: Addison-Wesley, 1974.
10. Taylor, Theodore. *The Cay.* New York: Avon Books, 1969, 144.
11. Torrance, E.P. "Guidelines for Creative Teaching," *High School Journal,* 1965, 459-464.
12. Torrance, E. Paul. *Guiding Creative Talent.* Englewood Cliffs, New Jersey: Prentice-Hall, 1964, 97.

CREATIVITY IN SECONDARY SCHOOLS

Jo Brazell
Carmel, California, Unified School District

The age of the moon shot, technical know-how, and the computer is also the age of educational frustration—frustration on the part of the educator who would like to have the time and the opportunity to teach; frustration on the part of those students who would like to become more involved in the educational process; and frustration on the part of those who find the educational process too difficult, too overwhelming, and too often, nonmotivating.

CONTEMPORARY PROBLEMS

Schools are crowded and demands are increasing, just as funds seem to be decreasing. The teacher sometimes becomes involved in schizophrenic role playing—taking the place of the parent, the minister, the doctor, and the counselor, with little time left for the professional role as the educator.

Today's educator of adolescents is also being placed in an awkward situation. In a relatively new role, the educator is expected to provide training in skills that will enable these students to hold jobs and to use materials that have not yet been developed. Thus the educator's duty is to provide the student with two skills: those needed to make a living and those needed to live an enriched life.

Because of pressures brought on by increasing amounts of subject matter and by an overflowing quantity of terminology, educators find themselves resorting to irrelevant and superficial questions that require "exact" answers: questions that deal with unimportant pieces of information; questions that encourage guessing without probing of statements, and questions that are ambiguous. A structure of this type seems to permit more to be covered in a shorter period of time and to be easier to evaluate. In order to relieve further pressures, a do-it-yourself movement of programmed and computerized packages seems to be infiltrating the market.

DEMANDS FOR RELEVANCE

The demands made upon the average adolescent student have steadily increased. The competition for college entrance and suitable jobs has become so intense that educators are beginning to see the need for completely reorganizing the educational structure. Education has become such a vast transcript of written material that even the most academic and talented student cannot begin to make a dent in it. What is relevant to the spectrum of skills today may be only unimportant historical facts in a few years. Because of these pressures, it has become increasingly important to train students to become both functional and creative readers.

Since today's students find themselves living in a critical period, classroom skills must become more than a veneer to education. They must become functional by helping the student to develop the ability to be a critical reader, to correlate and integrate information, to read between and beyond the lines, and to use the fullest extent the cognitive and affective domain.

A teacher needs all the help possible to teach each student to read the lines, read between the lines, read beyond the lines, and develop these necessary skills. Too often, one feels that team teaching, teaching aids, self-teaching machines, and materials will provide the individualized instruction that appears to be necessary for all children to succeed. Unfortunately, educators often overlook a resource group that needs specialized help—creative students.

CREATIVE EVOLUTION

Although creativity is the oldest recorded educational concept (the book of Genesis), the study of what constitutes creative thinking is still a pioneer venture. Too often, under the guise of creative dramatics or creative writing, the student is still faced with limitations of previous styles and with basic English rules imposed by the teacher.

Humans, however, are not just cognitive beings. They are sensitive to the existence of certain stimuli and react favorably or negatively toward them. Imagery, as well as emotion, is an important factor in the ability to grasp meaning. As a person encounters various situations, he or she begins to internalize values and to integrate attitudes into a total philosophy. Educators are becoming more aware of the fact that the senses are never fully developed to their capacity. To become more articulate, one learns many ways to say the same thing.

In dealing with the basic tool of the educational system—the book—the questions that an educator should ask are:

1. How can a student become flexible enough to use reading skills outside of the literature class?
2. How can students be freed from being tied to the literal word as they translate the author's message?
3. How can the student best be trained to detect the implied meanings presented by the author?
4. How can the student efficiently reorganize what is read into newly correlated and integrated concepts?
5. How can a student let imagination soar beyond the printed word in order to create new ideas never before expressed?
6. How can a student produce these reorganized and imagined ideas in concrete creations without the fear of ridicule when sharing the end product?
7. How can one train students to use cognitive maps as they make sensory searches?

Psychologists and medical doctors speak of "whole" persons and their experiences. If this is the case, students must be immersed totally in the educational process; must become aware that their education may come to them via different routes—visually, aurally, orally, kinesthetically—and must be motivated to learn and encouraged to share their knowledge.

Since reading skills enable each student to cultivate talents and develop self-realization, human relationships, economic efficiency, and civic responsibility, a functional and meaningful goal in the educational process is achieved by the educator who teaches these skills. Training one to use these skills, to transfer skills to other areas, to see the purpose of reading, and to develop self-motivation no longer limits education to a self-realization that occurs in the basic reading program from grades one to six. Instead, education becomes a lifelong avenue of skill building, application, reorganization, and creation.

To accomplish the training which will enable a student to become a functional, critical, and creative reader, teaching strategies must change. Teachers must use material that will enable the student to develop the ability to receive ideas, use them, test them, and throw them into fresh combinations. In other words, the teacher must help students develop the ability to interpolate, extrapolate, and project.

INHIBITORS TO CREATIVITY

Unfortunately, research in the area of creativity has focused on understanding the nature of creativity and the creative person, rather than on developing materials. There are inhibitors that affect the growth of creativity in the classroom. Education has become specialized. Students see subject matter as segmented; they do not see its relationships. Most of the educational texts are based on the lower realms of the cognitive domain that encourage convergent rather than divergent thinking. There is also a misconception that the "3 Rs" might be discarded in a creative curriculum rather than used as tools in developing higher skills.

Too often, by the end of the first or second grade, educators have instilled in students the fear that they are running a risk when they make mistakes. Students soon become reluctant to take chances, and begin to cling to accepted patterns. In order to get along, students must surrender themselves to being screened, classified, tested, scheduled, programmed, and conditioned by the school. This form of desensitization alienates the student from work and produces a nonmotivated student who either conforms or becomes a discipline problem. During twelve years in school, this student may become stereotyped, stamped, sealed, and delivered to society to play the expected role—that of a conformist. Or, as is currently apparent, the student may assume the role of a nonconformist without any guidelines at all.

CREATIVE REALITIES

How can educators, then, make creativity a reality in which the inner words audible only to the listening mind and heart can be brought forth to be shared and valued rather than remaining unexpressed, displaced, repressed, and finally obliterated?

Telling a student to read or write creatively is obviously futile. Students learn early not to take risks, and in creative reading and writing classes they may safeguard their security by expressing themselves in an incident which conforms to an approved topic, manner of expression, vocabulary, and length. Creative reading and writing must become much more than this form of approved recall. Time spans of remembrance, intimate emotional responses, complete grasp of memory—all must be reflected in the character of the work as the student reads and writes.

How does one go about developing a creative learning atmosphere? Readiness for germinating creativity could stem from the hierarchical arrangement of the critical thinking process. The teacher could develop materials to enable the student to go beyond commonplace education, which seems to encompass only knowledge and comprehension. Through the use of taxonomy, which would require students to look at the same material in many different ways, the student could be brought to maturity as a reader. These questions could deal with 1) basic cognitive goals (knowledge, comprehension, application, analysis, synthesis, and evaluation), and 2) the affective goals (receiving, responding, valuing, organizing values, and achieving a way of behaving which is characterized by a value system).

Two areas on the educational frontier attempt to induce creative thinking:

1. *Synectics* (The study of creative processes; the solution of problems in diverse ways.) This educational concept stresses spontaneous expression of ideas that are free from critical judgment.

2. *Morphological analysis* (The study of the meaning bearing units of the language and of how these units function; the formation of new words from internal elements of our language; the development of a communication framework.) This educational concept considers all possible combinations—even the coining of new words.

Although researchers may use different terminology, they agree that the most common characteristics of the creative process are fluency, flexibility, originality, and elaboration. Materials could be produced that would develop the student's ability to: write or draw in quantitative measures, adjust and adapt anything, rearrange and group words that are read, go beyond what has been written, create something novel, and add the needed unique details.

IMAGERY EXPANSION

One would think the head would ache from carrying around accumulating files of knowledge, audiovisual materials, and sensory aids. Although this is an absurd comparison, it is exactly what imagery does. Mental pictures or symbols are classified, stored, and recalled when the need arises or when a stimulus evokes a response. Imagination enables one to expand rather than to contract creative abilities. Imagery is so valuable and so economical—it is unhampered by lack of resources—that it should be investigated.

There are basically four kinds of creative imagery for which materials could be developed:

1. The ability to imagine oneself as the object or the subject.
2. The ability to study a process in order to create something new.
3. The ability to compare things symbolic through the use of metaphors and similes.
4. The ability to free the imagination from its normal boundaries in the form of fantasy.

Other creative language activities could include: developing open-ended sentences and stories; using day and night dreams as sources of language experience stories; recognizing a problem, analyzing it, suggesting possible solutions or consequences, testing it, and judging one's results; triggering responses that could arouse more than one sensory image simultaneously; and finally, playing with words and their meanings by rearranging, transforming, expanding, and reducing sentences.

Since historical situations condition creativity, since creative potential emerges when a student becomes totally immersed in a problem, since recurring themes can be placed in different contexts (thus dissolving already formed boundaries), since the arts can reflect feelings generated by environment, and since the arts are creative acts of symbolic languages, the humanities—now more than ever before—have a vital place in the creative curriculum.

MINIEDUCATORS

Education must be meaningful to students. They must feel included in curriculum planning and totally involved in the general educational process. The ability of the creative student to develop innovative materials, to correlate and integrate curriculum, and to explain problems in a unique manner must be capitalized upon. The development of classroom miniteachers rather than classroom aides captures the creative energy found in every class and to some degree in every student.

Why would one train students to become "miniteachers"? The reasons will become clear after reviewing some of the general strategies available to the teacher.

The teacher focusing on the educational task often turns to technology as an aid in individualizing instruction. The amount of hardware and software on the market is overwhelming and the cost is high. Technology offers the teacher, who can't work with each child at the same time, a form of patient repetition. This repetition comes in numerous packages of skills called "computerized learning." Another program offers minute, detailed explanations with a built-in opportunity to immediately check one's answers. This is known as "programed learning."

Tape recorders make it possible to record one's oral discourse and play it back. Reading pacers and other speed machines can force the reader to keep reading or read more quickly. Although all of these machines and their supplementary materials have assets, something is still lacking. Since "no man is an island," students need to communicate. They need meaningful dialogue, in which to test answers, seek solutions to problems, evaluate and weigh what is being said, learn through meaningful discussion, and ask "why?".

A learner is like an athlete, drilling and repeating exercises until the skill becomes purposeful and almost automatic. Each new skill is a prerequisite for another step in the learning ladder. But the athlete cannot work up to excellence alone; the coach checks every move, offers suggestions, and encourages the athlete in failure and success. Unfortunately, the teacher may be unable to give the desired personalized attention at the time the student needs it the most. The school cannot supply a teacher for each child, nor would it be practical to do so.

This need, however, could be filled by a miniteacher who has experienced the same problems but, for some reason, has not experienced the same frustrations. Someone who has empathy with another student in a similar learning situation could fill this void.

These students seem to have the uncanny gift of explaining in their own language what teachers cannot. Often, however, when these students are called upon to help as tutors, the teacher stifles their creative abilities by imposing methods upon them.

Student tutors have other assets. They not only speak the same language, but also, because there is no generation gap, they face the problem on an even keel with the other student. Sometimes the educator unconsciously lets bias and experience interfere and either overwhelms the student with a multiapproach method or confuses with an oversimplified explanation.

One tends to shortchange these tutors, however, by denying them the opportunity of understanding some of the basic philosophy of education and the rationale for using certain materials and methods. Operating in the dark makes these tutors less effective than they could be.

How does one train these students to become miniteachers with a sound educational background and yet allow them to explore academically, creatively, and individually the possibilities of teaching reading or any other subject in an innovative manner? In order to do this successfully, a sound methodology course must be offered to them by means of continuous inservice workshops. These workshops can be offered by district or country specialists, publishing companies, and local resource people.

The tutor is not a fill-in teacher and does not use a hit-or-miss procedure. The program, under the guidance of the teaching staff, must be structured and constantly reorganized and evaluated. The tutor must know what is to be expected of the pupil, know when the educational objectives have been achieved, know what experiences are necessary to achieve the objectives, know the pupil, and know how to evaluate the degree of change in behavior.

This means that the tutors work closely with the teacher. Developing this program is a slow process, but is worthwhile and necessary. Secondary students must become the key factor in this creative educational evolution: They have many of the same traditional basic facts under their belts, are still receptive to changes, and have the energy to practice innovations. This age group has ample time to develop talents throughout the secondary school years and the chance to establish a workable program. It also might be noted that this program could be critical in developing candidates for future teachers.

The teaching staff and resource people can train these tutors further by offering workshops in some of the following areas:

1. Art department—making and packaging individualized learning material into an attractive format.
2. Secretarial staff—instructing tutors on how to use some of the various machines for reproducing and organizing material; advising students how to use their time economically in order to work at a higher efficiency rate.
3. Physical Education department—developing a kinesthetic approach to learning.
4. Music department—preparing visual tracking exercises and auditory approaches to learning.
5. Math department—applying readability formulas to textbooks. This is valuable in understanding the independent level, instructional level, and the frustration level in reading; and it is also valuable in knowing how to place a student.
6. Publishers—presenting the philosophy of the program and demonstrating the special approaches necessary in order to elicit maximum response from the students.

7. English and Social Studies departments—developing in the student an awareness that written and spoken language varies in structure depending upon the situation.
8. Foreign Language department—instructing tutors how to use the listening lab with their students in order to get practice in oral reading, in replay of tape with critical analysis, and in listening to imitate proper phrasing and expression. These tapes would also help the tutor and the teacher as they plan more individualized instruction for the student. To facilitate diagnosis of specific skills that need to be developed, the tutor could be instructed on how to record in consistent form the mistakes made by the pupil in oral reading.

Each of the above groups of resource people can also be helpful in developing skills and technical vocabulary specific to each content area; in developing methods of reading each subject's symbolic language; and in creating innovative games, drill material, and tests.

SUMMARY

If one is to use creativity in an effort to make curriculum and educational changes, one must attempt to meet the following educational challenges:

1. To immerse the student totally in time-space creative activities, a cross-fertilization of ancient ideas with modern concepts may prove to be necessary.
2. To develop the primary source of creativity, imagery and ideational flows, methods must not rely solely on talent, socioeconomic conditions, and motor skills.
3. To develop functional reading skills, previous skills must be regrouped, reorganized, and used in new situations.
4. To develop a readiness for creativity, a hierarchy of critical thinking/reading skills must be established.
5. To develop the complete spectrum of creative imagery, one's personal analogy, direct analogy, symbolic analogy, and fantasy must be developed.
6. To develop motivation, attitudes must be changed.
7. To make education a cooperative lifelong adventure, giving of oneself to help another student makes learning a rewarding educational process.

PART THREE
MATERIALS AND RESOURCES

The task of *fostering reading growth* requires special materials and resources at the primary, intermediate, and secondary levels. Each chapter in this section indicates the differences of each level. However, education should be seen primarily as a totality of experiences. Thus, to assume that a certain content belongs permanently at one grade level and not at another would be contrary to the concept of individualization.

As principals and teachers adapt their programs to foster creative reading for the gifted, they will find helpful the stimulating ideas of specific materials and resources suggested for various grade levels. Recommendations for a creative atmosphere and a variety of materials to be made by teachers, pupils, and others should trigger countless ideas for adapting available materials to the differences in pupils' reading levels, skills, and interests. Requirements for bona fide creativity training activities and appropriate teaching strategies will suggest to teachers many ideas for specific activities suitable for their programs.

ML

FOSTERING READING GROWTH FOR GIFTED AND CREATIVE READERS AT THE PRIMARY LEVEL

Carl J. Wallen
Arizona State University

The most difficult and demanding task facing the primary grade teacher is also the most important—adjusting instruction to the individual differences of children. These differences range all the way from James, who comes to the first grade able to read the newspaper, to Tina, who cannot yet even recognize her own name. Contrary to popular practice, the adjustment is not best accomplished by using one set of methods and materials with children whose IQ is below 125 and another with those having IQs above 125. Some would suggest (10) that nongifted children should be given a basal reader method while gifted are given an individualized method. In commenting on programs for the gifted, Tinker and McCullough (11) noted that the activities described represent "good procedure for all children...." Bond and Wagner (2) pointed out that

> The adjustment of instruction to individual differences is more than a method. It is an attitude—an attitude in which the teacher assumes that each child has a right to progress as rapidly as he is capable, that each child can expect the school to provide for his rate of learning, be it slow or fast, and that each child can expect the school to study him as an individual and to help him when he is in difficulty.

The approach of using special methods and materials with special groups of children is related to the grade-conscious orientation that Austin and Morrison (1) identified in their study of the teaching of reading. They concluded that

> Too many elementary school teachers apparently have been unable to discard the concept that they are third or fourth grade teachers. Consequently, they feel compelled to teach the subject matter and skills which they consider suitable for their grade irrespective of differences that may exist

among children. These teachers expect all the children in their classes to read from the same page of the same book.

The current emphasis on special methods and materials usually results in poor education for the gifted because, in the opinion of Smith and Dechant (9), it is "extremely difficult to help the gifted achieve maximum growth under a system that must frequently be geared to the needs of the average or even the dull child."

The approach of relating methods and materials to special groups of children seems to be a symptom of a greater problem, materialism. Characteristically, we look to producers of material things to solve our nonmaterial problems. In considering the topic of reading and the gifted, we might avoid the usual consequences of our materialism if we begin with the basic goals of reading and then examine needs relative to those goals. We should avoid the rather natural materialistic tendency to ask, "What are the methods and materials that should be provided gifted children?"

READING GOALS

The basic goals of reading lie in two areas—cognitive and affective. In the cognitive area, we hope children will become skillful readers; in the affective area, we hope that they will use reading as a means of accomplishing ends that are important to them. Gifted children have special needs relative to the objectives of reading. Their cognitive development is so advanced that the materials and activities normally provided for children at their age and grade levels are so easy for them that they benefit little from instruction. Too, their affective development is generally such that they do not have to be motivated to read, in the traditional sense. All they usually need is time and a purpose.

Cognitive and affective goals are suggested. The goals are appropriate for all readers, not just those classified as gifted.

Cognitive Goals

The cognitive goals that have been identified as being appropriate for gifted readers vary from the suggestion of Gowan and Scheibel (4) that the only goal need be "increasing the reading rate," to suggestions that identify lists of objectives much like those considered appropriate for any comprehensive reading program (3, 6). The common element of the suggestions is a realization that gifted readers in the primary grades have usually mastered recognition skills—they are able to pronounce most words in a fourth or fifth level reading text—and so will benefit most from instruction for comprehension skills.

A suggested list of comprehension skills is drawn from two sources (12, 8). The abilities referred to in each are described in parentheses.

WORD MEANING
(Able to define and/or exemplify the meaning of specified words.)

PARAGRAPH MEANING

Recall
1. Recall-Identification
   (Able to recall specific items that were directly mentioned in the selection. The selection may be as short as a word or as long as a number of sentences.)
2. Recall-Organization
   (Able to organize specific items differently from the way they were presented in the story. The organization should reflect the relationship between specific items.)

Interpretation
1. Interpretation-Summarization
   (Able to identify the major idea presented in the entire selection or in a designated section of it.)
2. Interpretation-Conclusion
   (Able to identify underlying ideas in an unstated cause-effect relationship that can be logically inferred from directly stated items in the selection.)

Extrapolation
1. Extrapolation-Consequence
   (Able to use a previously identified cause-effect relationship to infer the consequences of changing either the cause or effect item.)
2. Extrapolation-Analogy
   (Able to use a previously identified cause-effect relationship to infer what an analogous one might be.)

Evaluation
1. Evaluation-Objective
   (Able to make judgments about the reasonableness or soundness of statements or events in a selection based on an internal criterion, such as supporting evidence, reasons, or logic provided in the selection.)
2. Evaluation-Subjective
   (Able to make judgments about statements or events in the selection based on a criterion external to it, such as one's own biases, beliefs, or preferences.

RATE
(Able to vary reading rate according to purposes for reading and the requirements of the selection.)

STUDY SKILLS

Location Skills
(Able to use pagination, alphabetization, indexes, tables of contents, and other organizing principles in efficiently finding information stored in telephone books, dictionaries, cookbooks, encyclopedias, fiction and nonfiction books, microfilm, card catalogues, and computers.)

Organization Skills
(Able to use outlining, summarizing, and note taking to put information in a useful order.)

Affective Goals

Gifted children may come to regard school with indifference or with positive distaste because they find nothing interesting to do there (5). A list of affective goals that might be appropriate is suggested.

SHARING
(Using special talents in individual assignments that are shared in some manner with the class.)

PLANNING AND ORGANIZING READING EFFORTS
(Developing discrimination, purpose for reading, and criteria for selecting books to read and enjoy.)

PURSUIT OF INTERESTS
(Having the time simply to enjoy doing things of interest.)

Considerations of goals for reading might be guided by what Sebesta and Wallen (7) suggest are the basic purposes for having reading instruction.

He who reads is able to negotiate his world with firmer understanding—to control some of the strands of his destiny: the long step from ignorance to wisdom. And he who reads is enabled to find surcease from the pressures inherent in our patterns of living. They are the age-old purposes given new hope: the purposes of knowledge and sanctuary.

SELECTION OF SUITABLE INSTRUCTIONAL MATERIALS

Growth requires challenge; this is the idea behind the developmental sequence built into most instructional materials in reading. To guide a child in developing reading skills, we provide books that are sufficiently difficult to be challenging. Matching book difficulty to a child's identified level of skill has been defined as *instructional level*; i.e., the child is able to pronounce correctly 93-98 percent of the words and is able to answer adequately 75-90 percent of the questions asked. This particular match of book difficulty and a child's skill is intended to provide an optimal setting for instruction because it encourages the child to grow in the use of reading skills.

Unfortunately, too few children are provided an appropriate challenge because their teachers take their cues from the labels on texts rather than from the children's individual skill development. Teachers too often assume that the number four on a basal text means fourth grade, and they assign texts accordingly. The tendency to read labels rather than children is illustrated in a study I conducted in 1970 of the basal text assignment of children. In school district A, the children were reading *above* the national average. In school district B, the children were reading *below* the national average. The teachers in both school districts provided the standardized reading achievement scores and basal text assignments of each child in their classroom. It was assumed that a child was reading at a suitable instructional level if the basal text assignment was no more than one year above or below the child's score on the standardized reading achievement tests. Thus, a child whose reading achievement score was 3.5 would be considered to be placed at instructional level if assigned to a basal text having a level of 3, 4, or 5; placement in a sixth level book would be considered at frustration level; and placement in a second level book would be considered at an independent level. Even with this wide range of instructional levels, about one-third of the children in district A (reading above national norms) were assigned books which were at the independent level, with almost no children assigned books that were at the frustration level. In district B (reading below national norms) the situation was just the reverse: about one-third of the children were assigned books which were at the frustration level, and almost none was given a book at the independent level. The same phenomenon would appear to be operating in both school districts: The teachers tended to assign children on the basis of grade level rather than achievement level.

The conclusion seems rather clear. If teachers are to provide instructional materials that encourage growth, then they must be ready to provide a variety of books at a child's instructional level. Many of the better readers, those we might call gifted, will require books two or more levels above their grade level. Some second grade children should be given sixth level books, and some sixth grade children should be given college texts. The teacher can better challenge the gifted reader to grow by basing text assignments upon achievement level rather than upon grade level. In addition to providing materials at different reading levels, the teacher should also make readily available a wide variety of printed materials, such as books encompassing various topics, children's encyclopedias, dictionaries, magazines, and weekly papers. But reading should not be confused with printed materials. All sorts of other-than-book media should be used to carry other-than-print messages. Audiovisual devices can play an important role in providing experiences for the child.

TEACHING FOR COGNITIVE GOALS

After providing the child with materials of an appropriate level of difficulty, the next task is to identify instructional exercises that are suitable for each child's specific skill needs. Teachers are seriously mistaken if they assume that a child's specific skill needs are directly indicated by a general reading achievement score; the score is only an average of subtest scores. The very process of averaging often hides the actual variation in subtest scores. For example, John's reading achievement score is 6.8; on the subtest for paragraph meaning he received 5.8 and for word meaning 7.8 which averages out to 6.8. Mary's reading achievement score is 4.3; her paragraph meaning score is 3.6 and her word meaning score is 4.9. The teacher should realize that even the subtest scores for paragraph meaning and word meaning are in themselves derived by averaging specific items. John's paragraph meaning score of 5.8 probably hides a wide variation in his attainment of the specific skills that constitute the large category called paragraph meaning.

When the teacher fails to identify the most appropriate instructional exercises for a child, and simply gives the exercises other children are receiving with the justification that a little review never hurt anyone, the teacher is committing an error that is commonly made with gifted children. Even a little review may hurt children since children are always hurt when not learning. They are hurt because they are not gaining new skills, which they can use just as much as any other child; and they are hurt because a rehashing of old material is uninteresting. What the gifted child needs is what all children need—instruction that is appropriate for particular needs. A good way to provide instruction appropriate for specific reading skills needs is to use a criterion-referenced approach.

Criterion-Referenced Approach

Criterion-referencing is relating the activities of testing and teaching to specific skill objectives. It is accomplished by designing a test and a

lesson for each specific objective. For example, there would be a separate test and lesson for each of these specific objectives.
1. Recall-organization: literature, fifth level.
2. Evaluation-objective: science, third level.
3. Rate: social science, fourth level.
4. Extrapolation-analogy: literature, sixth level.

The test for each specific skill objective is given; children receive the lesson for the objective only if they perform inadequately on the test for the objective. In this way the teacher provides a child with only those specific lessons that are appropriate.

With a criterion-referenced system, teachers orient instruction to the child's learning rather than to their own teaching. Because many teachers are oriented to their own teaching, they have a difficult time accepting that a child could attain an objective like *Evaluation-objective: science, third level* without ever having been taught it. Gifted children learn many things without formal teaching. The capacity for independent learning is, after all, what makes them gifted. The teacher's challenge is to identify reading skill objectives a child has not already attained independently.

A number of criterion-referenced reading systems are presently on the market, and one or two more appear each year. But teachers need not depend upon publishers to produce criterion-referenced systems; they can develop their own. Many teachers have developed effective criterion-referenced reading systems by cooperatively following a procedure of 1) identifying a suitable list of reading skill objectives; 2) assigning teachers to design tests for certain objectives; 3) assigning teachers to design lessons and identify suitable instructional materials for certain objectives; and 4) producing tests and lessons in sufficient quantity for each participating teacher to have a complete set. The major advantage of teachers developing their own criterion-referenced system is that they will be the master of the system they develop. Teachers familiar with commercially produced criterion-referenced systems are well aware that they are usually so complex that the teacher has a difficult time remaining the master of the reading program. Havelock Ellis once noted that the greatest task for civilization is to make people rather than machines the masters.

A criterion-referenced approach can be used with any method—individualized reading, basal readers, language experience, programmed, or whatever may be invented next year. A criterion-referenced approach is used when four steps are followed (*13*).

1. Identify a specific performance objective.
2. Test the children to identify those who have not already attained the objective. A child who performs inadequately on a test designed for an objective needs instruction.
3. Teach those children who showed that they need instruction for the objective.
4. Retest to make certain that the children have attained the objective and, if some have not, provide additional instruction.

The four-step procedure can be used with any method or set of materials the teacher happens to be using, whether commercially published or teacher made.

When teachers use a criterion-referenced approach in teaching reading skills they have a very clear idea of what each child is learning; and if they maintain records of children's attainment of those objectives, they can demonstrate that learning to principals, fellow teachers, parents, and to themselves.

TEACHING FOR AFFECTIVE GOALS

Cognitive goals differ from affective goals in that the former generally refer to products while the latter refer to processes.

Cognitive goals can usually be operationalized into performances that are testable: Reading achievement tests provide global measures of children's attainment of cognitive goals and a criterion-referenced approach depends upon an operational relationship between objectives and children's performance. But affective goals can seldom be operationalized into identified performances; to do so usually invalidates the goal. How, for example, does a creatively written story differ from one that is not? Creativity is a process and as such is not easily reducible to products.

In organizing instructional experiences appropriate for affective goals, the emphasis should be on the process of children doing activities rather than on what they produce in an activity. For example, children might be encouraged to visit the library and select books that interest them and then be given time during the school day to read these books. The teacher who really wants children to *read for enjoyment* (a process) will not introduce a product measure such as a visual display of the number of books each child has read: "Read twenty books and reach the moon."

Teachers often face a conflict in organizing learning centers when they must decide whether the centers should be for affective or cognitive goals. Does the teacher want the child to learn *something* or simply to be *involved* in the process of learning? Does the teacher want the child to read twenty books or read for enjoyment? Seldom are the two objectives compatible. A child reading for enjoyment may select a book so large that the contest is over before the book is finished. The child interested in getting to the moon will select short books that can be skimmed quickly and then claimed as accomplishments.

One advantage of using a criterion-referenced approach for cognitive goals is that it provides concrete information about children's learning, so the teacher is usually more willing to let children spend time in process activities that do not result in products that can be graded and taken home. And the parent who has seen records of the specific reading skill objectives the child has attained is more willing to tolerate the fact that the child seems to spend a lot of time "just fooling around" at school.

SUMMARY

Adjusting instruction to the individual needs of children is a difficult and demanding task for the teacher. It is particularly difficult with gifted children because the materials and methods developed for average children are inappropriate for the gifted. But the solution does not lie in identifying the materials and methods suitable for gifted children. Rather, it is best accomplished by using a criterion-referenced approach in achieving cognitive goals and in emphasizing process in achieving affective goals.

References
1. Austin, Mary C., and Coleman Morrison. *The First R: The Harvard Report of Reading in Elementary School.* New York: Macmillan, 1963, 81.
2. Bond, Guy L., and Eva Bond Wagner. *Teaching the Child to Read* (rev. ed.). New York: Macmillan, 1950, 61.
3. DeBoer, John J. "Creative Reading and the Gifted Student," *The Reading Teacher,* 16 (May 1963), 435-44.
4. Gowan, J.C., and R.W. Scheibel. "The Improvement of Reading in Gifted Children," *Educational Administration and Supervision,* 46 (January 1960), 35-40.
5. Hollingworth, Leta S. *Children above 180 IQ.* Yonkers, New York: World Book, 1942.
6. Murphy, Geraldine J. "The Education of Gifted Children: Suggestions for a Philosophy and a Curriculum," *School Review,* 62 (October 1954), 414-419.

7. Sebesta, Sam L., and Carl J. Wallen. *The First R: Readings on Teaching Reading.* Chicago: Science Research Associates, 1972.
8. Seymour, John, and Carl. J. Wallen. *Paragraph Meaning: Study Skills.* Albany, Oregon: Albany Printing, 1973, 2.
9. Smith, Henry P., and Emerald V. Dechant. *Psychology in Teaching Reading.* Englewood Cliffs, New Jersey: Prentice-Hall, 1961, 392.
10. Spache, George D., and Evelyn B. Spache. *Reading in the Elementary School.* Boston: Allyn and Bacon, 1977.
11. Tinker, Miles A., and Constance M. McCullough. *Teaching Elementary Reading* (3rd ed.). New York: Appleton-Century-Crofts, 1969, 110.
12. Wallen, Carl J. *Competency in Teaching Reading.* Chicago: Science Research Associates, 1972.
13. Wallen, Carl J. "Independent Activities: A Necessity, Not a Frill," *The Reading Teacher,* 27 (December 1973), 257-262.

FOSTERING CREATIVE READING AT THE INTERMEDIATE LEVEL

Robert E. Shafer
Arizona State University

MATURATION TASKS

In *Developmental Tasks in Education,* Havighurst (4) proposes that a period of life called "middle childhood" ranges from about 6 to 12 years of age and is characterized by three great outward pushes: 1) the thrust of the child out of the home and into the peer group; 2) the physical thrust into the world of games and work which requires the development of neuromuscular skills; and 3) the mental thrust into the world of adult concepts, logic, symbolism, and communication. Havighurst further proposes that by the end of middle childhood the individual has worked out a particular style and level in all three areas. Havighurst pictures the beginning of this period as a period of great potential where, within the child, untold resources are waiting to be realized through the unfolding powers of body and mind and through learning experiences from interaction with society. Havighurst proposes that the tasks are as follows:

1. Learning physical skills necessary for ordinary games.
2. Building wholesome attitudes toward oneself as a growing organism.
3. Learning to get along with age mates.
4. Learning an appropriate masculine or feminine role.
5. Developing fundamental skills in reading, writing, and calculating.
6. Developing concepts necessary for everyday living.
7. Developing conscience, morality, and a scale of values.
8. Achieving personal independence.
9. Developing attitudes towards social groups and institutions.

Independence and Creative Reading Skills

Almost all of the developmental tasks listed by Havighurst are related to reading instruction in the intermediate years. Space does not permit the exploration of the many varieties of implications stemming from current research in human development which ultimately will affect reading instruction. We might more profitably consider the implications of this research for the development of specific skills necessary for independent and creative reading of gifted young people attempting to achieve these developmental tasks in the middle years. How can reading help them?

We might look briefly at the middle childhood within the total area of human development as we consider the role reading is to play in it. Piaget has noted that with respect to the development of thought in the child—from the stage of egocentric and rather inaccurate thinking at the age of the beginning of school through the age of "concrete operations" in middle childhood and on to the beginning stage of "formal intellectual operations" from 12 to 14 years—the child passes through various phases of interaction with the environment, including school. All of this interaction facilitates development through a particular stage. Piaget (11) further notes a logical development of thinking based on the experience provided by the same physical and social environment which can be affected by skillful teaching.

Developing Concepts

With respect to the development of intellect, a child ready for school already has several hundred concepts—mainly the simple ones learned in the home such as roundness, sweetness, redness, dog, food, anger, love, mother—and uses these concepts as the tools for thinking. Along with other aspects of intellectual, social, physical, and moral development occurring in middle childhood, the child forms several thousand concepts. If these concepts are true to reality, a good share of them grow out of the child's concrete experience. The growing child stores up concepts and becomes able to form new concepts on the basis of vicarious experiences afforded by reading, listening, or seeing films. For example, a considerable amount of research has been done on the development of Havighurst's task, "developing conscience, morality, and a scale of values." Piaget proposes that at birth a child has no conscience and no scale of principles. Values are food and warmth. As the child learns values and to distinguish between "good" and "bad," the basis for conscience is the parents' punishment combined with acts of love and reward for the child and the child's love and dependence on them. Through the process of identification with parents or taking the role of the parents, the child develops the warning and punishing voice of conscience. From this time on, the child carries a controlling force at all times. Morality, or a respect for rules and behavior, is imposed first upon the child by the parent. Later, according to Piaget, the child learns the rules that are necessary and useful for playing games or carrying on any cooperative enterprise and therefore learns a "morality of cooperation or agreement," which is a true moral autonomy necessary in a modern democratic society. Piaget believes that the middle years of childhood are crucial in the development of learning this morality of cooperation. Development of morality and values implies development in an individual of the ability to choose between various objects and modes of action. The growing child must develop a scale of values in order to make stable choices and live by these choices. Piaget (12) has proposed that the development of a scale of values by which a child makes choices proceeds very slowly, but by the age of twelve the child is expected to be more able to make a considered choice than a young child seeking immediate satisfaction of every whim.

Lawrence Kohlberg has developed a theory and a program for describing stages of moral development somewhat akin to the kinds of stages which Piaget proposed for all aspects of human development. Kohlberg (8) describes moral development as taking place through three levels which he calls "preconventional, conventional, and autonomous or principled." He proposes that progression through these levels depends on experience and on formal education. He specifically notes that culture teaches the child through interaction with the family, peer group, and other social pressures, such as those within the school by such means as punishments and rewards, examples by teachers and culture heroes, and other similar influences. Kohlberg proposes that teachers present moral problems and dilemmas to students to encourage effective thinking about moral problems. He suggests that higher moral judgment will result and that the student will develop a solid self-concept which will provide support at the level of autonomous and principled moral behavior.

Maslow, Rogers, and other students of human behavior and human development have made similar proposals, but the implications for reading instruction and the impact of reading on the achievement of personal independence and the development of conscience and morality, as well as the impact of reading on other developmental tasks, have been only randomly studied. We need much more longitudinal research of the type done by Loban (9) if we are to understand the ways in which individuals pass through various stages of human development, since each individual passes through the various stages with unique language, culture, and experience in developing a self-concept and a personality.

READING AS AN ASPECT FOR LANGUAGE

Challenging Individual Growth

We know that growth and maturation continue throughout life. There are periods of time in the development of the individual when the growth is more dramatic and the manifestations of rapid change are more obvious. The years of growth encompassed by the public schools are without question the most dramatic during the period of middle childhood—the intermediate and junior high school years. Grades six, seven, eight, and nine are, almost without exception, the grades in which boys and girls are doing some of the most important growing of their lives.

The periods of preadolescence and adolescence have too often been thought of as merely the transitions from stages of childhood to adulthood—periods in which little of importance happens. It may be, as Kohlberg, Piaget, Chomsky, and others are proposing, that growth in all areas of development (physical, social, emotional, mental, and moral) is so rapid during these years that unique individual problems of growth will be more likely to arise. The values, attitudes, and beliefs that young people form during these years are likely to be lifelong and will in large measure determine success or satisfaction. They may determine what the individual will give to or take from life. Therefore, the intermediate school and the junior high have unique functions because they must provide for boys and girls who have unique individual problems.

Reading can and should play a vital part in this growth. The reading program must fulfill individual growth functions if it is to provide the kind of experience that will stimulate the individual growth stages. As we have seen in alternative schools, a new curriculum is being formed to include experiences which will stimulate students both in school and out. Instead of deschooling society, society is even more strongly involved in schooling, if not educating, children, as Postman and Weingartner have recently noted (13). This fact has led to an increased search for a viable relationship between school and community in American society. McLuhan's concept of a "classroom without walls" is coming true in many communities. What does this mean for reading?

Materials and Resources

What specific reading materials and resources in the intermediate schools will stimulate the growth and development of preadolescent boys and girls? Many times, certain children stand out as being superior students but we seldom know how superior and in what ways. This is unfortunate if there is truth in the theory that to be really "clever" in the sense that our British colleagues apply the term in education, one has to begin young. Alfred North Whitehead called it a need for "initial momentum." Tutoring took care of John Stuart Mill in this situation: he was taught Greek at the age of three. Michaelangelo, over his father's objection that such work was for artisans, spent his days as a sculptor's apprentice at the age of thirteen and by fifteen shared the company of Lorenzo the Magnificent and his guests, the most able minds of Europe.

Perhaps with our direction toward alternative schools and classrooms without walls, we will soon be able to apprentice some of our most gifted young people to engineers, artists, or physicists—a challenge which might provide the specific resources in reading that the gifted would need to pursue their special gifts. Malcolm X, in his autobiography, describes the development in prison of his own individualized reading program, while he ranged back and forth through classic and contemporary works in the prison library in an effort to find the answer to the dilemma of racial relationships in our country.

Unfortunately, in most schools we keep our gifted youngsters studying what they already know and marking time in basic readers in the elementary schools and in required reading courses in English, social studies, and other secondary school programs. Sometimes when they reach for the knowledge they need, they are told to wait; that knowledge will be forthcoming in another book or perhaps in another school. We need more exploration of the known intellectual facets of giftedness such as openmindedness, motivation, tolerance of uncertainty, preference for complexity, high regard for learning, and a sense of destiny. Such criteria are embedded within Havighurst's developmental tasks and demonstrate themselves in classrooms through manifestations of originality, spontaneity, and flexibility as well as the individual's attempts to search for meaning in various situations and to make meanings for her or himself.

Developmental Psycholingustics

That a child begins in the very earliest stages of language acquisition to build meanings from experiences has become an important idea in what Frank Smith, Ken Goodman, and others have called developmental psycholinguistics. Although the cooperative work of psycholinguists and reading specialists has become well-known, it is perhaps wise to summarize their definition of reading; this may indicate the kinds of programs and resources we need in schools if we are to develop the abilities of the gifted and to develop additional creative readers. In his essay, "Behind the Eye: What Happens in Reading," Goodman (3) defines reading.

- Reading begins with graphic language in some form: print, script.
- The purpose of reading is the reconstruction of meaning. Meaning is not in print, but it is meaning that the author begins with when he writes. Somehow the reader strives to *reconstruct* this meaning as he reads.
- In alphabetic writing systems there is a direct relationship between oral language and written language.
- Visual perception must be involved in reading.
- Nothing intrinsic in the writing system or its symbols has meaning. There is nothing in the shape or sequence of any letters or grouping of letters which in itself is meaning.
- Meaning is in the mind of the writer and in the mind of the reader.
- Yet readers are capable, through reading, of reconstructing a message which agrees with the writer's intended message.

Reading is a complex process by which a reader reconstructs, to some degree, a message encoded by a writer in graphic language.

Fluent Reading Skills

For the gifted student this search for meaning may be an even more dramatic characteristic of development than with other children. If one looks only at the development of reading skill, we can say that, by the time that most of the students we classify as gifted reach the intermediate school or junior high, perhaps half find the process of reading to be interesting or rewarding. Many of these children learn to read before they enter the first grade. Many master the encoding/decoding process and are able to use reading either to gain knowledge or for pleasure, perhaps by the age of eight or nine. Nevertheless, a large proportion of children are not stimulated by their elementary school reading programs; and, as we know from the controversies over "individualized reading" and "sequential reading" during the 1950s, many gifted children are "completely turned off" by the basic reading program. These children respond much more positively to individualized programs, wherein they are able to develop a continuing interest in reading, as well as the skills necessary to use reading for an extension of their own knowledge and for the achievement of various development tasks.

In his book *Understanding Reading: A Psycholinguistic Analysis of Reading and Learning to Read,* Smith (16) notes that decoding skills will be of very little use to the reader who has developed what Smith calls *fluent reading.* The development of fluent reading in the gifted child and in all children should be given our highest priority in our new reading program. We need to look carefully at our target before we develop programs and resources. Smith suggests that our target is the development of a child's innate quality as an information processor:

> Man is a creature who devours information. He spends much of his waking time selecting and acquiring information—and a good part of the time he is asleep organizing it.
>
> Man uses all his sensory systems for acquiring information which he integrates and stores in his brain. In the brain, man constructs a model of the world. The model is a summary of all his past experiences and a basis for all his future activity. In fact, it is not possible to separate the past from the future in either the brain or behavior, because in both the ongoing activity reflects past experience and future expectations.
>
> Man's appetite for information can be regarded as a constant search for regularities in external events—regularities that both explain the past and predict the future. The regularities economize on mental effort because they summarize experience and minimize the necessity to remember a multitude of individual events; they provide the basis for rules for deciding when two events should be regarded as being similar or different. Every discovery of a regularity of application of a rule is an instance of uncertainty reduction. As we shall see, the construction of rules for allocating events to a particular category is an important aspect of learning to read.

Smith goes on to point out that the implications of the work of linguists, psycholinguists, and reading specialists who have attempted to study the relationship between language and reading focus on the regularities of language and how a knowledge of them is developed by the child. Essentially, they see reading as an aspect of language, only superficially different from the comprehension of speech, because many of the skills in learning the regularities of spoken language are relevant in learning to read. The basic process is the same: the child attempts to reduce uncertainty and to discover regularity. Smith maintains:

> The point of view just expressed is so different from the way we usually view language perception that it will take a little adjusting to. But we are going to be very deeply involved in the view that reading is not a matter of going from words to meaning, but rather from meanings to words. To read words effectively, you need to have a good idea *in advance* of what it is that you are reading. This is not as paradoxical as it might seem; broadcasters, for example, like to glance through bulletins before they read them because they know it is much easier to enunciate the words appropriately with prior knowledge of the meaning. The question of what meaning actually is, or what comprehension can be, will be approached and then evaded...before considering how the receiver might get from raw sound or print to meaning, a function that we have already attributed to grammar.

INDIVIDUALIZATION

This concern for turning reading instruction around so that we start essentially with the individual and the ability to make meanings, rather than with a basic reader in interaction with the environment, is leading us not only to alternatives in the organization of schools and school curriculum but most certainly in reading programs. What are the implications of this change in focus?

Involvement

In *Language and Learning to Read: What Teachers Should Know About Language,* Hodges and Rudorf (7) give us the beginning of an answer. They quote the communication model of Ruddell and Bacon (14) which encompasses reading, listening, speaking, and writing and focuses on the processes of comprehending oral and written messages: decoding strategies, meaning strategies, and interpretation abilities.

Ruddell and Bacon pay particular attention to the interpretation aspects of the communication model, since they propose that it is by interpretation as a process that the reader (or listener) derives meaning from communication. This process of the derivation of meaning is, they assert, a function of experience, memory, and the skills involved in critical and creative thinking. Taking into account the work of Goodman, Smith, and other linguists and psycholinguists working on the relationship between language and reading, we should be extremely careful in applying such evidence to the development of specific materials and resources for instruction, without duly taking into account the consequences for children.

Further evidence for caution is supplied by Henderson in "Linguistics, Thought, and Reading" (6). In his paper, Henderson describes an incident which occurred in a demonstration reading lesson as follows:

> Thirteen or fourteen years ago, I think it was in the spring of 1957, Russell Stauffer taught a demonstration reading lesson with first grade children before a large audience at the University of Pittsburgh. The story was about children who were looking for a penny they had lost while playing in the park. Stopping the readers at this point in the story, Stauffer asked, "How do you think it will end?" All but one child, a boy, agreed that the penny would be found. Then they read to test their prediction. When all were finished, a girl spoke first, "We were right," she said. "They found the penny."
> At once the boy who had challenged the prediction...asked for the microphone and replied, "How do you know it was the same penny?"
> "No. We were right," said the girl, "and I can prove it." She turned to the last page of the story and read aloud, "They found the penny." Then she added, "If it had been just any penny, it would have said a penny."

Henderson concludes from this incident that the interplay between language and thinking which exists in the reading process, even in the reading of young children, is so infinitely complex and individualistic that any proposals for resources and materials not developed for specific individuals are simply irrelevant in school reading programs. Particularly with gifted children, we can see this incident multiply itself in depth and complexity in the middle years and we can also see the necessity for resources and materials which develop prediction, hypothesis testing, and substantiation judgment in both younger and older children.

Relevance

We face a great dilemma in the development of specific materials and resources. If children make up their own meaning and, as Smith and Goodman point out, go from meaning to language rather than language to meaning in learning to read, is it not necessary to provide them with situations both in school and out which will allow them to develop their own meanings in an individually stimulated atmosphere, at least for a part of the school day? Is it not also essential that such development be centered more than ever before on the individual's personal interests as best we can find out about them? Without attempting to be definitive in answering these questions, since I would propose that they merit a great deal more research attention than they have received, I cite the work of Niles (10). In her studies of instructional materials for reading, she has discovered important connections between materials and teachers:

> Many teachers will indicate that they could do a much better job of implementing a reading program if they had better materials. Probably they attach too much importance to materials—good teachers can and often have taught children to read well with very poor materials, even with materials far too difficult for the children. The *sine qua non* is the teacher, not the book.
>
> However, good materials make it easier for the good teacher to do what *could* be done with poorer materials; improvements increase the mileage teachers get from equal expenditures of time and energy. There are three categories of materials to be considered: 1) materials intended specifically for the teaching of reading, 2) library materials, and 3) content area materials. There have never been so many new materials in each of these categories as have flowed from the publishers in the last two or three years. Two major developments have changed the complexion of many of these materials. The first is the strong emphasis on relevance for today's children and youth. Many teachers feel that difficulty of materials, to which so much attention has been paid in the past, is less important than this relevance. In fact, some feel the lack of relevance may be a major cause of the difficulty. The second trend is toward a multimedia approach.

Relevance is very difficult, if not impossible, to define briefly. We usually think of it as related to interests: a story, for example, is relevant to a group of students if it deals with situations or ideas which they perceive as meaningful and important to them. However, in another sense, materials are relevant if they are expressed in a language which coincides with the language which is familiar to the readers. There has been much discussion of late of the irrelevance, in this sense, of the language of many basal readers. The rationale for the use of the experience approach to early reading depends in part on this matter of relevance of language. Good experience charts are expressed in the actual dialect of the pupils who create and use them.

If we consider the word *relevance* in the way Niles has used it, with special concern for the development of gifted and creative readers, we come ultimately to the question: "What stimulates reading anyway?" The child stimulated by relevant materials throughout the years of middle childhood may well accomplish all of Havighurst's developmental tasks to a considerable extent and also pass through the various stages of growth noted by Piaget and others. This child may come to be the kind of reader I observed when commuting each day by train. Each morning I would leave at approximately 7:30 a.m., boarding the train with a group of fellow commuters (mostly males), all headed to work in the center of New York City. I began to notice that most of my fellow commuters exhibited a number of characteristics of mature readers as described by Gray and Rogers in their classic study, *Maturity in Reading.* Their reading approach suited their purpose, and the material was relevant to their purpose. They were usually reading the *New York Herald Tribune,* the *New York Times,* or the *Wall Street Journal.* Their reading patterns were relevant to their developmental tasks. For example, those reading the *Wall Street Journal* would open the paper to the stock market quotations, scan until they found a particular stock, and read carefully the opening and closing quotations. They would then scan for stories about stocks that they were interested in on other pages of the paper and carefully read them. They would skim other articles of interest, and at exactly the time the train reached Grand Central Station at 8:10, they would have completed the reading job relevant to their purposes. I made similar observations of readers reading the *New York Times* and the *New York Herald Tribune.* Morning after morning throughout the years of 1962 and 1965, I observed their reading patterns carefully. Similar observations can undoubtedly still be made. Niles might note that relevance for these particular gifted and creative readers existed in the three newspapers.

Relevance to "Saturation"

What about relevance in specific resources for children in the middle years of intermediate school and junior high? I would cite two further examples: One is that of the experience Daniel Fader described in *Hooked on Books* and *The Naked Children*. In *Hooked on Books* (1) Fader asks himself:

> But what happens when the materials used in classes for the general student are selected to meet the practical needs of the student rather than the more abstract needs of the subject? In English, for example, rhetoric takes precedence over grammar, and utility becomes more important than beauty. When such criteria become the new basis for selection of materials, a radical change is inevitable. For example, such extremes of the same language as Shakespeare and the daily newspaper are found to have much in common. In terms of the practical needs of the student, the newspaper takes precedence. Because it begins more nearly where he is, it may prove to be the bridge across which he crawls, stumbles and finally walks erect, to where he should be. If he finds Shakespeare at the other end of the bridge, then the simple, inelegant newspaper, magazine, or paperback book has become a legitimate and necessary means to attaining a complex, eloquent end.
>
> When the goal of the English class is redefined in terms of rhetorical ease and willing expression, the ancient methods of the schools become as irrelevant to the subject as they have generally been to the student. Ease in understanding newspapers and pleasure in reading magazines cause both to replace the grammar texts and workbooks of time-dishonored usage. Instead of a student who spells according to rules, we may now have a student who spells by the image of words which have a hundred times impinged on his reading consciousness.
>
> Because the reasons seem as compelling as those for asking teachers *in every classroom* to teach English, the second part of this program is based on the principle of SATURATION, meaning the replacement, whenever possible and in whatever classroom, of customary texts and workbooks with newspapers, magazines and paperbound books. The object of this is to stir the sensibility of the practical child. Even as he learns to be reticent in a world of words he cannot fathom, so may he learn to be receptive in a world of words he can understand. Because he finds newspapers, magazines and paperbound books in every classroom, and because he *can* and *will* read them, he may yet be brought to compromise with a verbal world he cannot avoid.

Undoubtedly, many of us know the success story of the saturation approach in the Maxey School and in Detroit's Northwestern High School. But these were senior high school students, some might argue; and in some cases they were from socioeconomic and ethnic groups in a rural and an urban community where perhaps some would lack the stimulation of having many books in the home and sharing them with someone who is interested. But saturation and individualization worked here for Fader. Will it work elsewhere? In *How to Survive in Your Native Land,* Herndon (5) tells the story of how he and his two colleagues, Eileen and Arpine, decided to redo the reading program of their school in California. In talking about the seventh and eighth grades, they stated:

> So in the beginning of the school year 1968, we agreed to really teach reading. In the days before school started we—Eileen, Arpine, and I—pooled our combined vast knowledge on that subject. We figured it would be considerable, and indeed it ought to have been considerable. Arpine had never taught before, but she'd just come from courses in reading and children's lit with at least one first-class person at S.F. State; Eileen had already taught reading at a number of different places; I was (since my book came out) a big-shot educator who appeared on TV and was asked to give talks on what was wrong with the schools.
>
> In fact, it soon became clear to us that we didn't know a damn thing for sure. I mean, Eileen knew how to go in there and Teach Reading; she'd done it before and hadn't gotten killed or anything and she could do it again. Arpine knew a lot of books kids were supposed to like, had heard a lot about motivation, and had read Sylvia Ashton-Warner. All I really had in my head, as it turned out, was that if you got a lot of books around and didn't do anything else, the kids would end up reading them. I also knew that that wasn't true. It might be true in some other situation (like in my head or someone else's head) but it wasn't true in this particular seventh and eighth grade school which happened to be where we were. One or two kids would read them, one or two kids would write...in them, one or two kids would throw them, and the rest of the kids would ignore them; that was what would happen right here.
>
> After a couple of days and after a hundred coffees and a thousand cigarettes and a million words and quite a few lunchtime beers we were able to agree that we didn't know nothing. With that we all (I think) quite happily knocked it off, went home for the weekend, and were ready to start.

READING AS AN ART

Capsule Reviewing

After attending a conference with Herb Kohl and others, the three decided to make a complete survey of what was known throughout the field of reading and then to attempt to apply the best that was known and said to their particular students in their school.

> So there, the next year, Arpine and Eileen and I were embarking upon the revolutionary idea that teachers ought to know something about what they were doing. And there was Herb, yet another year and a half later, allowing as how that was so. It amounted to this: *no eye, no hurricane.*

We opened up with testing the kids, determined to try everything once and for all. We had a perfect situation for doing so, for grouping them on the basis of the tests, and for seeing what difference it made, since we were able to test them all individually and handle them in small groups afterwards. We gave an Oral Reading Test, determining from it not only something called Grade Level in reading, but also fitting them into categories according to what kinds of reading difficulties they might be having—i.e., they read well but didn't comprehend, or the reverse; they misread simple words, or inserted words which weren't there, according to context; they had troubles with certain sounds, diphthongs, consonants...we had a checklist of this kind of stuff and followed it through. After a couple of weeks of this we had our eight groups of seven to eight kids apiece, both Arpine and Eileen teaching four periods of reading each, each group about as rightly and rationally and scientifically placed according to grade level and kind of reading problem as you could imagine, short of only having one kid in each group. At the same time we were getting these books out of the library, and consulting with the special reading teacher about what she'd done with many of the same kids last year and getting the district language consultant down with her advice and help with materials and methods, and interviewing salesmen who called on us with this and that workbook, machine, book, classroom magazine or newspaper, drill system, skill developer...we read those pamphlets and books that no one ever looks at, things like *Guidelines to Reading, Reading Development in the Elementary Child, Motivating Reading for the Underachieving Student, The Case for Reading,* the kinds of books held in state college and district education libraries with three authors (the titles of the above are all made up, since who can ever remember them?) and we read Holt and Warner again and we read Tolstoi and I hauled out Bloomfield's marvelous neglected book and we would have read *Reading, Existence and the Absurd, The Zen Method of Reading Improvement,* or *Up Against the Wall Reading Teacher!* if we could have found them (5).

Problems of Review

Herndon, Eileen, and Arpine noted a number of "peculiar things" about the testing. They noticed that many of the students came out much lower on the individual or oral test than they did on the schoolwide test, and they also noticed that many of the children who were already gifted and creative readers and who were reading books like *Black Like Me* or Trevor-Roper's books about the Nazis or histories of World War II were pegged by the tests as third or fourth grade level readers. They also noticed that test results were extremely vulnerable to the conscious or unconscious influence of the test giver; that if the test giver's job or reputation depended on the improvement of the children, or if the test giver wanted the children to improve, it was likely that they would improve on the test. There were other problems about the testing, all of which have been written about before. In any case, after a thorough review of current readings in methods and materials proposed for intermediate schools, they concluded (5):

> Briefly, we just knew it was absurd that a normal OK American kid of any class or kind of twelve years old shouldn't be able to read. Why was it? Because reading is not difficult. Anyone can do it. It is an activity which no one seems to be able to explain but which everyone can do if given a chance. It is simple for people to do. If you know enough to tie your shoe and come in out of the rain, you can do it.
> If you can't do it, you must have been prevented from doing it. Most likely what prevented you was teaching. For one thing, if you have to get taught the same "skills" for seven years over and over again, you probably get the notion that it is very difficult indeed. But more important, the "skill" involved in reading is at once very simple and quite mysterious. Once you can look at *c-a-t* and get the notion that it is a clue to a certain sound, and moreover that that very sound which you already know means that particular animal, then you can read, and that is certainly quite simple, even if the ability of humans to do this is opaque. What you probably need to do then is to read a lot and thereby get better at it, and very likely that's what you will do, again, if no one stops you. What stops you is people teaching you skills and calling those skills "reading," which they are not, and giving you no time to actually read in the school without interruption.

Conclusions of Review

What Herndon and his two colleagues were finding out was that their students were having trouble going from print to meaning, instead of from meaning to print. As Herndon himself put it, "They were always practicing up to read, and the practice itself was so unnecessary, or so difficult, or so boring you were likely to figure that the task you were practicing for must combine those qualities and so reject it or be afraid of it." What specific materials and resources did they decide upon, and what did they find that worked? Not so strongly, Herndon's description (5) sounds very much like that of Fader's "saturation" reading program.

> Somewhere along the way we knew that what we knew about how to teach reading was what our memories could have told us, what we always knew, and that was that reading is best taught by somebody who can already read and who knows and likes the kid—the kid's mother or father or uncle or tutor or teacher—sitting down with the kid with a book and reading to the kid and listening to the kid read and pointing out things about sounds and words as they go along. That in the past everyone had known how to do that as part of being a parent or an uncle or an older brother and so everyone still knew, if they just wanted to remember it. That the "problem" of reading was simultaneously caused and invented by schools and their insistence on teaching

"classes" and "groups"—and by the resulting quest of teachers on finding ways to "teach," i.e., ways to standardize and to measure. That there simply is no way to measure what is crucial about reading a book—namely whether the kid liked the book, whether he imagined himself involved in the adventures of Jim Hawkins, whether he was changed by it. "This should change your life," says Rilke. Who can measure that? And yet it is all that counts.

So we were caught curiously in the middle. We were in a school which hoped to measure and standardize everything, and in which the kids themselves knew that everything important got grades, could be measured, and was standardized. No one was getting A's for being moved to tears when John Silver took off for the last time in the longboat. What we had to do was recreate the way of teaching reading which existed before schools were invented, and use it in the school itself. Reading not as a skill (to be measured), but as an art (that which changes). Nothing could have been simpler. Get a lot of books in the room, tell the kids to bring their own, go around during the period and sit with each kid for a couple of minutes and let him read a bit to you, read some to him perhaps, talk to him about the book and what's going on in it, point out (perhaps) this and that word, sound, and then let him go on and read it while you go over to the next one. Say over and over again—in the classroom, in the teachers' room, in your sleep perhaps—A good reading class is when the kids come in with their books, sit down and read them, and don't stop until the bell rings. Resist the urge to talk and discuss, resist the urge to watch the kids all happily working in the workbooks and programmed materials, resist the urge to motivate and to teach something to everyone at the same time, resist the urge to measure one person against another or everyone against any standard; resist every day all the apparatus of the school which was created in order to enable you to *manage* and *evaluate* a group, since it is just that management which destroyed the kids you have in your class.

Herndon continues saying that the above method words for, as he calls them, his eight, hardline nonachievers at Rabbit Mountain School as well as it does for the "regulars." He says it works in school terms according to standardized tests, it works in terms of the teacher's observation, and it works in terms of the parents' observations of the students; and to the students' own surprise, since "having battled themselves for so long about reading, they wanted it, when they came to face it, to be a more heroic task."

> It worked. I knew it worked because by the end of the first year I stopped hearing all those complaints about reading class. I stopped hearing kids ask me for passes to get out of Reading, to go here and there on some important errand which had to be done during reading period. I stopped hearing about how awful Eileen was and how mean Arpine was. I even heard the dreadful admission that someone was looking forward to going to Reading, looking forward to reading their book, looking forward to a little peace and quiet where they could be left alone and *do what they wanted.*

SUMMARY

There is much more to Herndon's story of *How to Survive in Your Native Land,* but his case study of the teaching of reading in the Rabbit Mountain School may help us to come full circle through the studies of developmental tasks by Havighurst and the work of the developmental psycholinguists, such as Goodman and Smith, to the relevant resources and materials to develop fluent meaning in reading and ultimately to those qualities of giftedness—such as open-mindedness, motivation, tolerance of uncertainty, preference for complexity, high regard for learning, and sense of destiny—present in the creative individual in various dimensions of fluency, originality, spontaneity, and flexibility.

If these are our goals, then we need to change our methods and resources in reading in the ways suggested above. If we are able to do this and do it soon, we may ensure that passages through the years of middle childhood and adolescence are not merely physical processes but that the social processes involved in Havighurst's developmental tasks become what Friedenberg (2) called for more than a decade ago when describing the fundamental task of adolescence as defining "clear and stable self-identification." Friedenberg further pointed out that, if we were able to develop a culture which helped each adolescent begin this definition, we would not be faced with the "pliability" of life in our society and the "dangerous and troublesome prospect" that few youngsters really dare to go through adolescence, that they merely undergo puberty and simulate maturity. It is to the creation of the fully human adolescent—the adolescent who faces life with love and defiance—that we need to dedicate our new reading programs, and indeed, our schools as well.

References
1. Fader, Daniel, and Elton B. McNeil. *Hooked on Books.* New York: Berkley, 1966, 16-17.
2. Friedenberg, Edgar Z. *The Vanishing Adolescent.* Boston: Beacon Press, 1959, 2.
3. Goodman, Kenneth S. "Behind the Eye: What Happens in Reading," *Reading: Process and Program.* Champaign, Illinois: Commission on the English Curriculum, National Council of Teachers of English, 1970, 5.
4. Havighurst, Robert J. *Developmental Tasks in Education* (3rd ed.). New York: David McKay, 1972, 19-35.
5. Herndon, James. *How to Survive in Your Native Land.* New York: Bantam Books, 1971, 134-137, 140-141, 143-145.
6. Henderson, Edmund H. "Linguistics, Thought, and Reading," in Richard E. Hodges and E. Hugh Rudorf (Eds.), *Language and Learning to Read: What Teachers Should Know About Language.* Boston: Houghton Mifflin, 1972, 169-188.

7. Hodges, Richard E., and E. Hugh Rudorf. *Language and Learning to Read: What Teachers Should Know About Language.* Boston: Houghton Mifflin, 1972, 169-188.
8. Kohlberg, Lawrence, and Turiel Elliot. "Moral Development and Moral Education," in Gerald Lesser (Ed.), *Psychology and Educational Practices.* Chicago: Scott, Foresman, 1971, 139-145.
9. Loban, Walter. *Problems in Oral English: Kindergarten Through Grade Nine.* Champaign, Illinois: National Council of Teachers of English, 1966.
10. Niles, Olive S. "School Programs: The Necessary Conditions," *Reading Process and Program.* Champaign, Illinois: National Council of Teachers of English, 1970, 66-67.
11. Piaget, Jean. *The Language and Thought of the Child.* Leuchatel-Paris: Delachaux and Niestle, 1923.
12. Piaget, Jean. *The Moral Judgment of the Child.* New York: Harcourt Brace Jovanovich, 1932, 55.
13. Postman, Neil, and Charles Weingartner. *The Schoolbook.* New York: Delacourte Press, 1973.
14. Ruddell, Robert B., and Helen G. Bacon. "The Nature of Reading: Language and Meaning," in Richard E. Hodges and E. Hugh Rudorf (Eds.), *Language and Learning to Read: What Teachers Should Know About Language.* Boston: Houghton Mifflin, 1972, 169-188.
15. Shafer, Robert et al. *Success in Reading,* Volumes 1-8. Morristown, New Jersey: Silver Burdett, General Learning Corporation, 1973.
16. Smith, Frank. *Understanding Reading: A Psycholinguistic Analysis of Reading and Learning to Read.* New York: Holt, Rinehart and Winston, 1971, 28, 34-35.

CREATIVITY TRAINING ACTIVITIES FOR SECONDARY SCHOOL STUDENTS

Joseph S. Renzulli
University of Connecticut
and
Carolyn M. Callahan
University of Virginia

Although research has consistently shown that almost all students can improve the quantity and quality of their creative output, many secondary school teachers experience a great deal of difficulty when they attempt to encourage youngsters to express themselves creatively. Part of this difficulty is due to group pressures toward conformity that typically exist among adolescents, but the problem is also a result of our failure to teach students the basic skills of creative thinking. All too often we have assigned students higher-level creativity tasks without first providing them with the underlying techniques that are necessary for more complicated assignments such as writing expressive poetry, creative stories, or imaginative essays. The purpose of this chapter is to point out some of the basic techniques for encouraging youngsters to think creatively. The first part of the chapter will deal with the general strategies for developing creativity training activities. This will be followed by brief descriptions of some specific activities that can give students practice in creative thinking.

PRINCIPLES UNDERLYING CREATIVITY TRAINING

The Fluency Principle

Research in creativity training has shown that the more ideas a person generates, the more likely that person is to come up with new and unusual ideas. For example, when a group of students was presented with the hypothetical problem of thinking up a name for a new breakfast cereal made from dandelions, almost all of the students called the cereal "Dandy Flakes." Since creative ideas are, by definition, unusual or infrequent solutions to problems, and since "Dandy Flakes" was the response given by more than 90 percent of the students, it was judged to be a relatively common response. The teacher then asked the students to think of five more possible names for the new breakfast cereal. Needless to say, several unusual names were created, and in many cases, students developed names that were unique to the group. For example, one student suggested manufacturing the cereal in the shape of lions or lions' heads and calling the cereal "Dandy Lions."

This example helps to illustrate the fluency principle. Unless we encourage students to develop many ideas rather than just one, and unless we reward them for the sheer quantity of ideas they produce, they may never get beyond the ordinary and the obvious. Fluency training activities such as the dandelion problem give students practice in the basic creativity technique of brainstorming. Such activities are good warm-up exercises for more complicated activities because they help youngsters explore various alternatives to problems and thereby free their thinking processes from the restraints that usually hinder creativity.

The Principle of Open Endedness

The principle of open endedness is closely related to the fluency principle. Simply stated, creativity training exercises should not have predetermined answers. A good deal of the "educational game" played between teachers and students is based on the mental process of convergence. Teachers usually raise problems that have one solution and reward students for the speed and accuracy with which they converge on the solution. Such exercises provide students with very limited opportunities to let their minds reach across a broad range of possible solutions to a given problem.

Open ended activities also help students develop the skills of self-evaluation. When an answer is either right or wrong, the final source of judgment always resides with an external authority—usually the teacher or a textbook. With the threat of evaluation and the fear of being wrong constantly hanging over their heads, it is little wonder that students are reluctant to take risks and to express thoughts and ideas that are somewhat unusual or divergent. Open ended activities, on the other hand, provide youngsters with a psychologically safe atmosphere in which to express themselves. When there are no right or wrong answers to problems, and when students are given an opportunity to generate many possible solutions to a particular problem, the students review their own alternative responses and select the response that they like best. This is not to say that the teacher and other students should not have an opinion about the youngster's work, but students pass judgment on their own work and their opinions are valid since they are based on their own standards and criteria for self-satisfaction.

The Principle of Environmental Relevancy

Students engaged in creativity training should not be penalized for a lack of knowledge about a particular topic. In other words, creativity training activities should allow learners to draw upon their own backgrounds and experiences. For example, if we asked youngsters to engage in "thing listing" by writing all of the things they might find in a kitchen, they would not have to search through reference books for responses. Although this is an open ended exercise based on experiences common to all youngsters, it also helps to make adjustments for differences in background and ability level. Youngsters from affluent homes might list garbage disposals and microwave ovens, but even students from so called disadvantaged homes will be able to respond within the limits of their own experience. And while less able students may focus mainly on concrete items, brighter students may include certain intangibles, such as pleasant aromas and the warm atmosphere that they might associate with a kitchen.

As has been indicated above, the major purpose of warm-up activities is to give students practice in generating several ideas and solutions to a given problem. Unless these activities are relevant to a student's present background and immediate environment, the exercises are likely to become traditional search for information experiences. The major purpose of developing brainstorming skills can easily be lost if the student is asked to slow down divergent thinking processes in order to search out factual information. Thus, creativity training exercises must be based on information that is relatively common to all members of a group and at the same time, be open ended and allow for many responses.

The Principle of Enjoyment

Creativity training, like any other aspect of the teaching-learning process, can become a routine and dreary experience if we do not guard against the forces that tend to stifle enthusiasm and enjoyment. Even the most exciting activities can lose their appeal if they are administered in a mechanical fashion by unenthusiastic teachers. One of the best ways a teacher can demonstrate genuine interest in creativity is to become an active participant in training activities. When the teacher shows a willingness to reveal creative thoughts and ideas, contributes to class discussions on an equal basis with students, and is not afraid to operate in a free and open atmosphere, students will quickly develop trust in the teacher and feel secure in situations which reward unusualness. It is one thing to tell students that we want them to strive for originality, but it is much more effective to display the kind of behavior that we want to elicit from students.

Whenever teachers and students are purposefully striving for unusualness, a good deal of laughter and humor is likely to occur. The teacher must accept these reactions (especially laughter directed at the teacher's creative ideas) because humor is an important part of creativity. Attempts to suppress laughter will invariably result in a dampening of the free and open atmosphere that is necessary for the development of uninhibited expression.

Students will also derive more enjoyment from creativity training sessions if they have an opportunity to participate in planning the activities. While we hear a great deal of talk about cooperative planning, much of what goes on in classrooms is solely determined by the teacher. Once students have been exposed to a variety of creativity training exercises, they should be given a choice about which types of activities they would like to pursue. Since the objective of such activities is the development of creative thinking processes rather than coverage of subject matter, creativity training exercises provide an opportunity for students to deal with topics that are of interest to them. For example, adolescents can practice brainstorming by listing of all of the possible names for musical rock groups. If students are interested in politics or ecology, they may want to write slogans or design symbols that promote their points of view. Capitalizing upon student interests will help to maintain enjoyment and enthusiasm and, at the same time, will shorten the communication gap that often exists between adolescents and their teachers.

CREATIVITY TRAINING ACTIVITIES

Creative Writing

As has been indicated, creativity training exercises are designed to help free students from the usual constraints that are placed on their thinking and thus prepare them for higher level assignments such as creative writing. Numerous activities can be developed around brainstorming and thing-listing formats. In preparation for creative writing, students can develop lists of words that are related to given emotions such as fear, happiness, and sadness. They can also be given the stems of common similes such as "as big as _____" and "as quiet as _____" and asked to develop several colorful comparisons that will complete each simile. Similar exercises can be developed for analogies and metaphors. In each case, it is important for students to generate as many responses as possible for each item. Students can also apply the brainstorming technique to developing lists of synonyms and antonyms for given words. Additional word fluency exercises can be carried out by asking students to write specific ways of conveying a certain meaning. For example, there are several dozen specific ways of communicating the act of speaking (say, bellow, whine, mumble), each with its own special meaning. Students will gain greater control over their writing when they learn to explore a wide variety of possible words to create a certain mood or feeling.

Word-listing activities can help prepare students for writing poetry. Before introducing rhyming patterns in poetry, the teacher can ask students to list all of the words they can think of that rhyme with a given word. This exercise will generate a great deal of excitement if carried out under mildly competitive conditions. Students can compete individually or in groups to develop the longest lists of rhyming words. They can be introduced to rhyming patterns such as those used in limericks and use words from their lists to write original limericks.

One of the problems that teachers often face when attempting to develop creative writing abilities is helping students generate interesting ideas for their stories. Brainstorming and thing-listing exercises help students find ideas. For example, students can list ten or twelve roles or characters in the first of four columns on a piece of paper, numbering each item. Characters or roles might include astronauts, clowns, or deep sea divers. The second column should list places: the inside of a fallout shelter, a jungle, an underwater cave. The third list should contain actions: swimming, building an igloo, chopping down a tree. The final column should list objects: teapot, television antenna, broom. After all of the lists have been completed, students should randomly select one item from each of the four lists, by rolling a set of dice or using a spinner, to use as the elements for a short story. Forcing relationships among things not logically related may result in some interesting and unusual stories. Students can use their lists several times, and the activity can be varied by placing certain specifications on one or more of the lists. For example, the list containing characters might be restricted to famous people or characters that students have encountered in their reading or the actions list restricted to occupations or recreational activities.

A similar technique can be used to help students develop interesting character sketches. Categories of physical characteristics such as weight, height, age, eyes, hair, and build can be written on a piece of paper. Students should be asked to list as many words or phrases as they can think of under each category. For example, under the age category, students might list *baby, girl, teenager, old man*. After students have listed as many words as they can under each heading, one item should be randomly selected from each list and the words used as the basis for a character sketch. Needless to say, some unusual and quite fanciful characters will emerge from this technique and this will help students break away from the formula type of characters that often result when students are not given practice in combining characteristics that are sometimes incongruous. The main purpose of this technique is to help youngsters stretch their imaginations by providing them with an exercise where unusual relations are forced together.

The brainstorming and word-listing techniques can also be used to help students develop the skills of descriptive writing. Students can list words associated with each of the five senses. For example, under the sense of touch, they might include *smooth, rough, mushy*. After students have completed their lists, they can write descriptive paragraphs that highlight some of the words on their lists. The paragraphs might focus on one of the senses or a combination. Students can also brainstorm a number of topics for description—a rainy afternoon or the midway at a carnival—and then write a description that incorporates perspectives on the topic from each of the five senses.

Figural and Symbolic Creativity Activities

One way of capitalizing on student interests and special talents is to combine figural and symbolic activities with verbal activities. For example, students might be asked to design a camper or a recreation park using given size specifications. When the designs have been completed, a number of verbal exercises are natural follow-up activities. Students might be asked to write slogans to sell the camper, a technical description of the park that would enable a landscaper to lay out the park, a classified ad for the camper, a political speech that would convince the town council to provide the funds to build the recreation park, or even a simple description of the camper or recreation park. One might also make use of special interests in art or music by asking students to write descriptions of moods created by abstract paintings or music played on a tape recorder or record player.

The close connection between symbols, emotions, and propaganda might be the basis for a thing-listing activity in which students are presented with pictures of well-known symbols such as the peace symbol, hammer and sickle, star of David, or United Nations symbol. They may list their emotional responses and then write an essay on how these symbols have been or might be used for propaganda purposes.

An activity in which students can create closely related verbal slogans and symbols for a business, club, or school team will often motivate the child with little verbal fluency but some artistic ability to complete a verbal task by its close association with a symbolic task. It is, of course, important that the teacher reward both efforts in order to emphasize the need for a fluency of modes of expression as well as fluency within a given mode of expression.

SUMMARY

There are a number of general techniques for encouraging youngsters to think creatively. The four basic principles underlying creativity training have been discussed. The fluency principle states that the more ideas a person generates, the more likely he or she is to come up with new and original ideas. Open endedness implies that creativity training exercises should not have predetermined answers; instead they should enable students to generate many solutions to a given problem. Environmental relevancy emphasizes that students should not be penalized for lack of knowledge about a particular topic. The principle of enjoyment suggests that enthusiasm is an important part of creativity and that a free and open atmosphere is necessary for the development of uninhibited expression.

These principles and the specific suggestions which followed were not intended as coobkook recipes for creative thinking or as formulas which in and of themselves will lead to the creation of brilliant literary works. However, the principles and the activities which develop from them do serve an important function in the development of the creative thinking process. They free the student from the traditional modes of thinking which call for a search for the one right solution and, instead, encourage exploring many possible alternative responses, drawing upon entire life experiences in searching for responses, evaluating one's own responses, and enjoying and feeling confident in expressing ideas to others no matter how real or unreal, true or fanciful, practical or whimsical, those ideas might be.

PART FOUR
MEETING WRITING NEEDS

Gifted students who read many content area textbooks and think about instruction in reading and writing in the content area, know the importance of the reading/writing connection across the curricula. What students read influences what they write. Therefore, this section provides the reader with sensible principles across the curricula that dramatize perception of reality and encourage spiraling creativity and nonlinear thinking.

By studying the writing and imagery process we can see the whole generic development and intellectual dialectics in gifted and creative. It is not enough to postulate theories about what we must give the gifted and creative to read, we must examine the actual dialogue, comprehension, and thought processes that reveal the true nature of gifted and creative from prewriting to fully developed discourse.

ML

WRITING AS REVELATION: FROM TELEPHONE BOOTH TO MACROCOSMIC VIEW

Michael Mathias
Seton Hall University

A DRAMATIZED WRITING ACROSS THE CURRICULUM APPROACH

Teachers have used creative dramatics to teach composition since at least 1969. Gallagher (3), for example, cites Mathias using the art forms of mural, collage, and film drama of artist Patrick Sullivan to stimulate dramatic improvisation. In this writing project, the students first studied wall murals of Sullivan's Irish ancestors, then studied the artist as a personality, and finally participated with the artist in dramatic improvisations.

In an attempt to unify theory with the field of process composition, I developed the theory of "figura." This theory suggests using body movement to generate comprehension and language processes. In *The New Theater and the New English,* I wrote, "The education of the artist (student) through visual hieroglyphs presents a new concept of education through the arts by preconscious figurations" (5).

From the figura theory, a series of principles of generative language development has evolved. This chapter presents the principles of generative language development: Imagery inspired by movement creates a style of thinking and a style of writing that can be related to a series of principles in a process. This process is represented here in a hierarchy, beginning with primal thoughts and spontaneous improvisations and moving to the gradual complexity of the research paper. The movement from expressive to transactional writing is documented in terms of body movement, imagery, and dialectic in the reading-writing process. A dramatized method of thinking is offered for developing prewriting, writing, and editing in an integrated curriculum (6).

THE PRINCIPLES OF GENERATIVE LANGUAGE DEVELOPMENT

Principle 1. The body encodes/decodes meaning through gestures, thus making images personal and allowing personal reactions to a text within the context of the student's experience.

    a. First, the students pantomime in imaginary environments. By imaginatively entering a metaphor and moving through the playwright's world, they can arrive at greater cognition and comprehension.

    b. In developing this prewriting principle, students identify their personal feelings and attitudes.

    c. By entering imaginary environments, they can develop a freedom of language as they attempt to write expressively.

    d. After watching films on the creative process, they can simulate interviews with cult heroes. Students could, for example, question Woody Allen on his sense of humor and relate it to their own sense of absurdity. Absurdity can give creative students a view of hidden values in reality by removing the masks and facades of false logic.

After viewing the film "The Mind of the Clown," Joseph created a diagram of unfolding doors (perhaps the doors to his first inward investigations). Above the diagram he wrote the following: "Where am I in relationship with humor. Well..ah..uh, I'm not really sure. I love Monty Python, and that's humor." The first insight Joe had was that his sense of humor is bizarre.

These first thoughts seemed to suggest to Joe that in order to develop humor, he needed to tear down Woody Allen and make him an alter ego. He then interviewed Woody Allen in a prewriting improvisation:

    Woody: Who's he?
    Me: A sci-fi novelist.
    Woody: Why do you think these people are funny?
    Me: I like chaos..the unexpected..the ridiculous.

Joseph criticizes Woody Allen as "silly," comparing him to his own idol, Monty Python. Notice that his self-realizations become stronger as Joseph begins to search for his own personal definitions of absurdity.

Activities such as Parachuting through Space in an Imaginary Dream House, or View of Reality As Seen by Living in a Telephone Booth, free the student to view reality from another dimension. As a result of one such assignment, one student wrote a short story mocking what he calls plastic material society: The telephone booth becomes a metaphor for the parasitic business world which drains the poorer class. In Stanley's use of body movement, he imagines himself squeezing into a confined space: "I was concentrating on the size and shape of the booth from about three yards away in the car. If you were too big, you probably had to extend your hand forward to reach the receiver, then dial." His dramatic perception emphasized the conflict of the body against the confinement of the glass booth: "I am no tank so I got inside quite easily. In ten seconds glimpse, my eyes had covered all the external features that made up the phone. Then with one look backward, I discovered that there was a little seat for relaxation" (6).

This same student subtly conveyed the theme of absurdity through the use of the figura from dramatic improvisations by contrasting his own body to that of a "Big Tank." He extended the metaphor of the telephone booth: a glass cage in which modern society continually oversees one's privacy ("two people on my both sides see my lips and hands going through motions, gesticulating"). This student learned to use gestures, use his body as the "actor's body." Like the playwright he later encounters, he conveys larger themes through "soft writing" first (1).

In contrast to the above activity, students can move the furniture to create space in the classroom where they can reveal personal images and reactions. Movement and gestures can awaken language processes. The energy that flows through gesture, mime, and physical characterizations later appears on paper—the process is very much like a free association webbing technique. Ideas are caught like butterflies in a spider web of unfolding dreams.

Principle 2. Through kinesthetic configurations the body outlines and surveys the unknown. The body represents these configurations as Visual Units or Metaphors. When students use mime to survey the text of an unknown author, the body suggests imagery which illuminates the metaphors of the author. The playwright conveys the themes of the play through the visual metaphors of the mise en scene, and so students can enter the author's world through sensory exploration, gesture and mime.

a. Delve into the playwright's world. Students might explore Beckett's Wasteland through gesture and mime, reacting to the setting. After such an experience, Anna wrote: "Every man carries his own little cross. It is his own burden till the day he dies. In light of this burden are the voices of the dead. Their voices sound like leaves rustling in the air. A rustling sound of leaves, to me, is a dreary lonely setting. It will creep into your system and bring you deeper into depression."

b. Students might listen and explore voices in the war games of *Loneliness of the Long Distance Runner* through gestures. Frank wrote:

"We could play for hours pretending to kill each other. No matter how many times we were killed, we still got up. We never though how horrible the game of war would be in reality with real bombs and bullets...."

c. Students might become the characters of the author, or they might write their own passages using the author's metaphors. In this prewriting exercise, Kathryn reacted to the central metaphor of the carousel in *Catcher in the Rye* by Salinger in the following way.

> The carousel like the world goes round. All the kids reach for the gold ring. I watch them..I watch Phoebe..Cyclic repetitions..the Incas, the Hindus, and even the ancient Chinese believed in eternal cycles. There was a birth out of the chaos of the Universe, an ascent, where all the creative processes were allowed to flourish, and then a decline back into chaos. The golden ring—the golden age—and have not men and even children struggled to grasp both?

d. Students might respond to the author's ideas in their own poetry and prose. The student begins to demonstrate comprehension by generating contrasts and comparisons between authors. Having encountered Woody Allen and Samuel Beckett separately, Maria was able to draw analogies:

> The image or mind of a clown is the center of absurdity. He is a nonhero, an antihero who represents modern man. The clown falls but returns to his feet. Woody Allen uses the clown image to satirize man's life....Beckett does the same thing as Woody Allen. He has Estragon and Vladamir talk at each other, but do they understand? They keep questioning their existence. They do not know why they are waiting.

David applied his own concept of absurdity from Beckett and Ionesco in a poem:

> Absurdity: man coming to terms
>   with this world
> Absurdity is the devaluation of language
> as a means of communication...
>   limitations in man's ability
> to comprehend all of reality in a single system of values
> showing the spectator the harsh facts of a cruel world

e. Students may criticize the author after reading first person narratives or autobiographies. In this essay, Jenifer compared Beckett and his mentor, the blind Joyce, to Hamm and Clov in *Endgame:*

> The final and most dynamic pair were Joyce and Beckett. Beckett was Joyce's personal slave. Beckett read to Joyce, was his best friend, and av-

idly studied Joyce's work. Beckett put Joyce on a pedestal, as if he were Christ. As Joyce was blind so was Hamm and eventually Pozzo. Lucky is the only one left to care for Pozzo but Lucky is unknowing. Throughout Samuel Beckett's writings, *Waiting for Godot, Endgame* and *Krapps Last Tape,* there are threads of regression involving his mother and the other women in his life.

f. The students then combine their earlier drafts—a series of process interrogations or dialogues with an author's ideas, images and conflicts—into a rough draft of a research paper. Students leave the telephone booth to question the author. The research paper becomes an extension of dramatic improvisations that began with the investigations of the mis en scene, the setting of the playwright's world. Students settle on a thesis only after a series of prewriting investigations. Forcing a thesis upon students makes a graveyard out of research: Students learn to fish out dead facts and arrange them in a preconceived order imposed by the teacher.

Gifted students need to feel that research comes out of the gestalt of discovery and investigation. Jenifer developed questions that led to her own thesis: "*Godot* left the audience and the reader wondering if Lucky would take over after Pozzo's blindness. The ending of *Endgame* had the same effect. Would Clov really leave Hamm, or would Clov get the boy out in the field and resurrect Hamm?"

Students individually and simultaneously participate in a silent writing workshop in the manner of the "loop writing process" (2). They are free to discover their own language insights in the author's texts. Only the students' own reactions and comments are reproduced for other members at each stage of the prewriting process. They arrive at theses during the process of interacting with imagery, as Richard did:

> Although Jung clearly cites the absence of archetypes, the essay contains evidence to the contrary. There are a series of contradictions in the text that suggest "archetypal backgrounds," but Jung, for some reason, refuses to analyze Ulysses as archetypal or as emerging from the unconscious.

Principle 3: Metaphor is the exploding dynamic of transformation as it follows the movement of the body through space and time, the transformation of one image as it moves forward into another. Students learn that metaphor is not static. They learn to extend imagery from improvisation in drama to the imagery of transformation in science.

a. Students might discover an absurdist metaphor for the nuclear threat such as "desks" for missile bases.

b. Students transform images of absurdity into images of researched facts on nuclear devastation.

c. The students learn that they can use metaphor in different areas of the curriculum and on different levels as well. For example, metaphors are effective on the physical level and the psychological level in science. Science becomes a dramatized perception of reality. The creative process continues when we move from a conflict of emotions to a conflict of ideas. From improvisations dealing with emotions students can move easily to conflicts surrounding ideas. Dialogue between characters can emerge as a dialectic between opposing ideas in science, for example. The dialogue on absurdity moves from a discussion of the wasteland in Beckett's *Godot* to an attack on the issues of nuclear devastation, but David is able to retain the sense of the absurd and apply it to the nuclear issue:

> Mr. Sec: As I said before, the President's desk is large enough to accommodate all our missiles.
> Woody: Then you are saying the President's desk is spread all over the world? Where do the desks of all the other world leaders fit into this puzzle?
> Mr. Sec: There are really only two large desks in the world today, theirs and ours.

A dramatized view of reality is evident in David's ability to convert the absurdist point of view from the section on drama into metaphors which involved his science research. He combined two strands of thought: the sense of the absurd from the exercise on *Beckett/Mind of a Clown* and research on nuclear war. Transformation of metaphor implies that the dramatist's image can be transformed into "imagery of atoms" which can be transformed into "universe, from cell to galaxy," which can be transformed into "the cell as metaphor for loneliness" for a sociology class, or "atomic age, the study of the time-line in American History."

After researching images of devastation, students recorded their impressions of physical destruction. Michael wrote:

> Extremely high temperatures which will melt down steel to its original form will follow, as well as burst of fire balls traveling at the speed of light which will leave only ashes in its path, causing blindness to those who dare to stare in its eyes.

Melinda dramatized inner conflicts by depicting psychological devastation:

> The mind would become immobilized, numbed, and seemingly deadened to the realization of what had happened. Destruction of family, personal belongings, and once familiar surroundings would be gone like a ghost in the night. The ability to function normally as an individual or as a collective group would be irreversibly altered. The mind would seemingly sever all pre-

viously existing social behavior patterns....The whole woven fabric of cultural societies would be liquidated.

Finally, Melinda defined the spiritual and metaphysical questions:

> Doubt in spiritual goodness of the "Almighty" (be He of any faith) would overwhelm aching, untrusting hearts. Places of worship and adoration would crumble to the ground leaving no institution for spiritual guidance or congregation. Was this His Plan?

Principle 4: The kinesthetic sensory motor activity of drawing a map or a graph is an extension of gesture, outlining metaphors of the unknown. The brain constructs visual metaphors prior to knowing. The teacher can use the stills of video frames as schema to elicit webbing, mapping and graphing ideas in the prewriting process. Graphing, in this prewriting process stimulated by video stills, is an extension of gesture. Just as gesture conveys meaning through movement in space, graphing from video stills extends comprehension. The visual metaphor suggests cause and effect relationships and a dialectic that emerges out of the descriptive writing. The following pattern of activities emerges: Video stills create visual metaphor; visual metaphor generates descriptive writing; and questioning processes emerge suggesting dialectic.

According to this pattern, students might base descriptive writing on stills of the sun during a major solar eruption, photographed in ultraviolet light from the Skylab orbiting space station in 1973 or the Orion Nebula giving birth to stars. The videotape of Carl Sagan's *Cosmos* is an excellent source of stills to elicit drawing, mapping, and webbing in prewriting activities. Descriptive writing (the second stage in the pattern) based on the images of frames of the Cosmos are expressive of a dramatized perspective. Marybeth wrote in a dynamic, colorful mode:

> We are floating through a seemingly endless black hole trying to fulfill human curiosity, and to develop our knowledge of the cosmos which is necessary for our future survival. The Cosmic black is magically interrupted by intricate patterns of diamond, topaz, and ruby studs shimmering as if they were attached to an enormous black velvety stole.

The students' questions that emerge out of their descriptive writing on the cosmos proceed from a conflict of ideas to the posing of dramatic questions. Melinda wonders: "Where do we come from? Is there a great creator? Do we know the bounds of space? Will we ever know?"

After looking at stills of the "spiral staircase" of the replica of the cell and DNA, students responded to their idea of the human as the creator of new gene mutations, or as the destroyer of the universe. Given excerpts from poems about the celebration of the universe, students can either celebrate the universe or create the attacking voice in prewriting exercises. The stills of the Cosmos videotapes created images which gave birth to a language of celebration for Victor:

> The day comes to us in the form of the morning dew. It travels on the sun's rays full of multi colors of yellow, red, and orange. God created the darkness, an infinite space full of deep silence where all the creatures of the world sleep silently. Now modern man has tried to out master God. Man has cracked the DNA code.

Creation of the Attacking Voice

Visual metaphors serve as a bridge between dramatic improvisations (a drama of ideas) and the posing of questions, assertions, and the creation of opposing points of view. Visual images create a dialectic in the writing process. Students can uphold the celebration of the universe or attack scientific theory. The attacking voice can be a dramatic voice.

The teacher can develop activities to orchestrate the attacking voice. For example, students might respond to the outdated theory of the Craniometrists of 1854. They compare Nott and Gliddon's *Types of Mankind* with statements made by Jefferson and Lincoln which contain racist overtones. Students comment on the scientific integrity of comparing diagrams of the black natives of Algeria and the Sahara to images of gorillas as a measure of the intelligence of the black race. Students are allowed to attack or support the false premises of pseudoscientific theory based on racism.

In another example, students might react to images from Michael Talbot's *Mysticism and Modern Physics* by drawing diagrams of Quantum foam, or of a "holograph" as described in the chapter called "Superspace." They can either support or reject the scientific truths of the "new physics." For example, Susan writes: "Man is totally responsible for himself....There is no beginning or end to humanity....Even coming straight from his mother's womb, an individual is his own person...."

On the attacking side, John asserts, "I feel we are but ants in a world of gargantuan creatures. We are little creatures, wiped out by one swipe of the creature's paw." The dramatic dialogue encourages students to discover their own reasons for the attacking voice. Scientific theory is taught as an extension of the absurd universe; curved space may be real or fiction; the theory of the "big bang" may, according to John, be an illusion like the arrival of Godot:

> Air, Clouds, Trees, Earth are all fallout products. We are the result of an explosion, a waste product. The fusion of many minute gases. Let's be realis-

tic. We are nothing but carbon or are we products of a supreme species, the after effect of a total wipe out. *Who are scientists to tell us* what is and what will be. How dare they base their hypotheses on something that has no factual basis. Who can you trust? Scientists? Please! Who created Nuclear Weapons? Certainly not Jack and Jill. The World came in a bang (so they say) and now it can go in a bang.

Integration with Sociology: "Loneliness in the City"

Students might be asked to transform scientific imagery into sociological metaphors. For example, the image of the cell can be transformed into a sociological metaphor for urban isolation. Vincent, for instance, extended the meaning of cell: "Each person is a cell, a part of the game. The cell loses its identity, but gains a new identity by gambling with its lives." The idea of using the cell in terms of social isolation is metaphoric and evidence of the dramatic consciousness of the student.

The dramatic voice is an assertive voice. Pati remarked that the improvisation in class using the ironic or sarcastic tone helped her focus on a tone in her writing. Students may be asked to read the same passage in several different tones and with intentions opposite to the literal meaning of the text. As one student commented, "The tone of voice in this reading changed the way I felt about it. It seemed that it was by a person disgusted by the effects of the war...."

The dramatic voice can assert its own power in every area of the curriculum. Vincent's growth in dramatic power and perception is revealed in his ability to use a metaphor from science and apply it to characterizations of people in an urban environment: "The lonely city is a massive board game....The old man's hands are sores, sores that never seem to heal....His hand lost its old identity, but gained a new identity through drugs." In this example the student moves from the literal statement of facts, the surface of description, to a mode of thinking that uses dramatic metaphor to state a sociological theme. This process shows a tremendous growth in dramatic perception in the use of literal description. The old man is on drugs; he is a victim; he is spiritually dead. Vincent cleverly conveys this in the mise en scène: "The apartment buildings are tombstones in a graveyard."

Principle 5: Visual metaphor is a natural thinking, conceptual process of the brain. The mind conceives of eidetic configurations before knowing. Cognition is a translation of visual metaphors into decoded propositions and units of meaning. The unfolding of metaphor is molecular and dynamic, initiated by the movement of the body as figurae through time and space. Metaphor is a movement of the mind formed after the movement of the body. When we look at a painting, a sculpture or a piece of architecture, the temporal order of our perceptions is static. When we look at a dancer moving through space, we are made aware of the dimensions of time: past, present and future. The movement of the body suggests a time line and imagery that is molecular. Metaphor is molecular because it is not static. Not merely a comparison, metaphor is in a constant state of transformation.

The transformation of metaphor resembles the body in motion; movement gives us past, present and future in a time line. The three aspects of time are joined in a single performing act. Metaphors developed in a collage of history in a time line reveal to the student a co-existence of past, present, and future. Comprehension is expanded with cause and effect relationships in the temporal order. Static metaphors can be given a molecular dimension by placing them on time lines or in a collage evoking past, present, and future.

Students may be asked to create sculptures out of objects that have special meanings for them. They can create collages on the walls and ceilings with images from the total class consciousness. For example, footprints walking on the ceiling may suggest a "journey through time of an individual life."

Students may be asked to bring in a Hindu lantern to cast shadows on the walls where collages of India's past, present and future suggest time lines and motifs for Hesse's *Siddhartha*.

Integration with History: Visual Collages of the Time-Line

The motor activity of creating a collage of images of recent American History based on cut-outs of Time Magazine's "America, the Last Sixty Years" is an extension of gesture. Images set in a time line of history suggest motion from past to present and from present to future. The placement of imagery on the collage, one against another is like the movement of the dancer. The eye darts back and forth between present and past and present and future, as if in a dance of unfolding comprehension. The violent and dynamic images of the collage generate a language of motion—a "kinesis" of language because the movement from paragraph to paragraph is filmic and is an outgrowth of the metaphors of the collage. Marie created a time line integrated with dramatic vision:

> I think, perhaps, negative conclusions cloud our perspective as we dwell on the bellowing clouds erupting in flashing sunlight, of mangled bodies strewn on a bed of red rivers and of dynamic individualists gunned down by Mr. Death before their time. I believe that the past is relevant and poignantly linked to the present as well as the future.

Students move into and out of the images of the collages; through improvisation comes a dynamism of perception in space and a dynamism in power of writing style. Marie turned her time-line into a dramatic fist to attack materialism in civilization:

> With the explosion of the atomic bombs, we entered a new era. Out of the amber fires that streamlined across the sky, skyscrapers reached out to touch the heavens. Technology exploded beyond our limitations and Judy Garland's "Somewhere Over the Rainbow" became a reality. But in the land of Oz and at the end of the yellow brick road, we Americans of today succumbed to the worship of too much leisure wrought about by autonomy. We relinquished our conceptualization ability to Space Invaders and waited for the person in front of us to be an individual or take a stance. This makes me think of the fall of Rome when ease and contentment were taken for granted *but the wrath of the Almighty crushed them out wiping contented grins from their faces.*

Curriculums for the Future

The concept of a curved space has influenced our thinking. We are no longer a linear thinking people. Linear thinking had only one possible goal—pathways leading ruthlessly to a fixed goal.

Thinking in the new age has become cyclical; space is no longer conceived as separate from matter. Indeed, not only is matter now viewed as oscillating in space-time, but even electronic particles are seen as interconnected with what Wheeler refers to as "superspace," or "quantum foam." Space is compared to "a carpet of foam, spread over a slowly undulating landscape...the continual microscopic changes in the carpet of foam as new bubbles appear and old ones disappear, symbolize the quantum fluctuations in the geometry" (7).

Sarfatti has elaborated upon Wheeler's imagery. He imagines the quantum foam as a "turbulent sea of rotating mini-blackholes and mini-whiteholes. Various electromagnetic and gravitational patterns are similar to the ripples created by a stone tossed into a still pond. Some of these may be protons, others, neutrons; the patterns interact to form atoms, which interact to form molecules, which interact to form the substance of the physical world. Thus, in some odd way, the stones and the stars are merely undulations in the nothingness" (7).

The concept of an undulating universe has been expanded into the concept of a universe as a giant hologram. A hologram is a three-dimensional image, projected by a moving object into space. When intersected by a laser beam, the hologram can be clearly seen in several dimensions. David Bohn, a physicist who worked with Einstein on the theory of relativity, has given us a totally new view of reality. We must build our writing across the curriculum programs on the new physics and "the new reality." Its implications go far beyond Einstein. Supporting David Bohn is a group of physicists and psychologists who are discovering an empirical language for proving not only that protons and neutrons of matter and space interconnected, but that consciousness itself may be a projection of this gigantic hologram.

What the mystics have told us about the interconnectedness of consciousness and reality is now the serious concern of scientific proof and investigation. The leading physicists have produced books on the subject which have created a chain reaction in modern intellectual and scientific thought. Frank Capra's "The Tao of Physics" has pointed out that the concept of an electronic particle as being both a point in space and a wave has created an entirely new concept of reality as being both part of space and time and part of an undulating continuum. The result is that the average person living in America will soon be bombarded and invaded when the mass media project the "holographic model" of the universe.

David Bohn and Ken Wilbur in "The Holographic Paradigm" point out that the mind, and, indeed, the brain itself may be a holographic projection of the universe, with each point of consciousness interconnected with the electronic particles of space and time, and indeed they may discover soon a causal relationship between the movement of electronic fields in the brain with the movement of electromagnetic fields in quantum physics.

If all this sounds like *Alice in Wonderland* for gifted students, it is! And what's more, everything that young people may love in science fiction films such as "E.T." and "Close Encounters of the Third Kind" is being confirmed and projected into the media by people of outstanding intelligence and brilliance. Their cultural impact is being felt in the field of the new physics and the new psychologists. We must incorporate these themes into the curriculum for gifted students. Gifted students are aware of nonlinear thinking and curved space. We cannot put them back into a telephone booth. We must shatter the glass and help them break out of the confinements of linear thinking and invite them into the "macroage."

The computer is bringing us a new solitariness. The computer, in demanding that gifted youngsters spend long hours with their mental landscapes, may help create an inner dialogue and new awareness of an increased spirituality in writing. The intense concentration on technological logic coupled with the increased practice of meditation is producing a trend in young people which may result in nonlinear thinking. Previously, young people had been under the domination of the square, the rectangle, and the pyramidal triangle. One starts at point A and is taught all through childhood that the phases of life are part of a progressive hierarchy leading to point B, the apex of the pyramid, the life's goal (being the president of a college or marrying a movie star like Marilyn Monroe).

In other words, we have concentrated on goal-directed, materialistic thinking for gifted, characterized and supported by visual symbols, like the rectangle and the triangle. However, the rectangle and the triangle suggest a boxed universe, a universe with limitations, a universe which is divided into linear segments of time. The tripartite analogy—beginning, middle, and end, youth childhood, marriage, and old age—has become an anachronism in the 80s. The linear curriculum must give way to a new approach to integrating writing across the curriculum that dramatizes perception of reality and encourages spiraling creativity and nonlinear thinking. In the 1980s I propose that we explore the use of different modes within the contexts of the new physics.

Let there be no dividing lines between the writing to images, the movement through metaphors of the author's texts and the images of the author's personal life, and responding to opposing points of view of critics. All of these processes take the students out of the linear line as Paul Connolly states in the article, "Soft Writing and Hard" (1):

> More importantly the procedure from "soft writing" to "hard" (and it is a process not a progress) is not linear but circular. That is, a writer does not simply ascend from observing to theorizing but must constantly circle back testing generalizations against particulars and building again from the record to the theory...the writing process may be imagined as a circle, not a line.

We are taking gifted students out of the linear process and putting them into a circular, spiraling process; we are taking them out of the telephone booth. Let us take our students on a journey of consciousness. Let us study the thinking processes of gifted students from first improvisations to dialogues that can release unlimited creativity and powers of expression, stimulated by the new physics and the integrated liberal arts curriculum. In addition, using concepts of ensemble, students can create an interior dialogue with literary geniuses such as Beckett, Miller, and Ionesco, without the intervention of a lecture. When we remove the linear concepts of classifying, students demonstrate through their writing an unlimited sense of power, imagery, and creative response.

At this time, writing is still being taught as a separate discipline across the curriculum, whereas I advocate a spiral approach: psychology, history and the new physics should be taught in the same creative manner through student encounters and prewriting improvisations. We should stress the importance of moving from drama of the absurd to a dramatized conception of the universe—a drama of ideas of the new science and its impact on the student's world vision. Implications of using the new psychology and the new physics in the classroom with gifted can change the nature of education in our country. Are programs for the gifted presently using ensemble processes in integrated arts curriculum? Or is the emphasis only on producing engineers and technological scientists? An international focus on the techniques of a dramatized interarts curriculum would release a nuclear explosion of intelligence and creativity in literature and the arts.

References
1. Connolly, Paul. "Soft Writing and Hard," unpublished essay, Bard College, 1983.
2. Elbow, Peter. *Writing with Power.* New York: Oxford University Press, 1981, 59.
3. Gallagher, Phillip. "Project Ten," *Spectrum Magazine,* 1969. Amherst: University of Massachusetts.
4. Martin, Nancy, and Robert Parker. *Writing and Learning across the Curriculum, 11-16.* London: Ward Lock International, 1976, 26.
5. Mathias, Michael. "The New Theater and the New English," unpublished doctoral dissertation, Rutgers University, 1974.
6. Mathias, Michael. "Principles of Generative Language Development," unpublished essay, International Reading Association Convention, Chicago, 1983.
7. Talbot, Michael. *Mysticism and the New Physics.* New York: Bantam, 1981, 77-79.

PART FIVE
SUGGESTIONS FOR MEETING UNIQUE NEEDS

One of the greatest potential sources of gifts and talents is the gifted child who, as measured by the standard norm, differs in clothing, dialect, or culture. To develop these gifts and talents we must provide learning experiences which reflect the values and make use of the real language of these pupils.

Growth will occur as each child participates comfortably in understanding how language works. Furthermore, by understanding his or her own interests, concerns, purposes, and extent of development, the child will be dealing with the essence of reading.

Motivation for meeting the unique needs of certain gifted and creative students may be accomplished through many avenues. One important training approach is called "make believe." As children try and test various ideas, they focus on feelings of others—both real and fanciful—through activities in art, rhythm, dramatization, and creative writing.

Educational problems that may lead to decline rather than growth are also discussed. Of particular importance are problems which are attributed to lack of educational reform, misleading ideas that gifted children do not need special assistance, and the immature mores of all parties concerned. These unique children are hindered in maintaining respect for individual variabilities, thus encouraging failure in learning. To prevent this failure, the needs of early and older readers are pointed out and a variety of reading programs and techniques is suggested. Ninety-five challenging enrichment activities are suggested for providing powerful instruments of learning in developing this unique, creative reader.

This section also focuses on putting positive theory into practice and thereby allowing equal emphasis for minority group, learning disabled, gifted, and creative children. The needs of this diverse, creative group are outlined. The schools overcome lack of success by developing the strong points in the special child rather than focusing on weaknesses. Finally, this section offers a number of activities that have been used successfully with special children.

ML

MAKE BELIEVE: AN IMPORTANT AFFAIR

Margaret S. Woods
Professor Emeritus
Seattle Pacific University

"What do you believe in?" The answers which satisfy youth may vary considerably as a result of human and environmental influence. Let's listen to one high school student who speaks eloquently for some members of her peer group:

> What do you believe in?
> Nothing is real
> Life's what you make it
> Come on Boy, deal.
> It's not your problem,
> The world and its hate
> But let someone else do it,
> You'll have a long wait.
> Burn up your draft cards
> Go march for peace
> Protest louder
> The guns will not cease.
> Mark my words
> You'll live to tell
> That being the minority
> Is worse than hell.
> What do you believe in?
> Nothing is real,
> Life's what you make it,
> Come on Boy, deal.

During a 200 year period, Toynbee (7) postulated, a great nation moves

> From Bondage to Spiritual Faith
> From Spiritual Faith to Great Courage

From Great Courage to Liberty
From Liberty to Abundance
From Abundance to Selfishness
From Selfishness to Complacency
From Complacency to Apathy
From Apathy to Dependence
From Dependence back again to Bondage.

Strong evidence suggests, however, that we are struggling to discover and create positive alternatives. Whether people will accept such alternatives will depend upon feelings gained from personal experience, whether they trust authorities as a result of these experiences, and upon research which validates such experiences.

THE VALUE OF MAKE BELIEVE

Among the earliest training events for every child, especially for the gifted child, are situations in which the child is entitled to make believe, to try out various ideas, and to test both real and fanciful worlds. A child encouraged to make free use of make believe might someday conjecture, "Just suppose monies which go into financing and launching a rocket were allocated instead for launching into life's orbit fully equipped human rockets." *Just suppose*—two words which help us to see the world as it is, to imagine what it might be like, and then, hopefully, to possess the courage and the know-how to change.

According to Toynbee, the one who learns how to use personal power to create is free at any time to save a situation by developing new techniques, new institutions, new ideas, new attitudes of the mind, and, above all, new states of feeling (7).

For some time, society has been coping with a crisis—all sense a need to yield new answers. Such skills, I contend, are learned and are being learned, some through the use of such simple words as *just suppose,* or *make believe.* Recently, in a "Lively Minds Seminar" participants from age 9 to 82 responded to the question, *"Just suppose* you could make this a better world for all people, what would *you* do?" An 82 year old replied, "In addition to having exchange students in other countries to develop a better understanding and acceptance of others, I would exchange the leaders of countries."

A high school student suggested, "I would have open house for all students the first two days, meeting with teachers, with registrations the third day with those classes taught by those teachers I knew would help me do the best job of learning."

A second high school student suggested an alternative: "I would have high school students sit in with the personnel director when prospective teachers are interviewed. As it is now, adults select the teachers but we spend the days with them."

I believe that skills for selection and for relating and responding are developed through *just supposing* and *make believe,* for then we see conditions as they are and as they might be.

THE MEANING OF MAKE BELIEVE

That powerful catalyst, imagination, has been recognized by the astute as the source which supplies the well-oiled machinery for maximizing the individual's potential. Einstein considered imagination to be more important than knowledge. Anatole France said, "To imagine is everything, to know is nothing at all." Holbrook (3) concluded that nourishment and exercise of imagination are the roots of true literacy in all.

Trevisa defined the power that we call imagination as the "Faculty for forming images whereby the Soul beholdeth the Likeness of Things that be Absent" (1). Fry (2) defined imagination as an "unborn or embryonic belief."

Observing children at play, some teachers and parents can usually recognize imagination at work in all make believe activities, which Isaacs (4) called "Nature's means of individual education." Through the use of make believe, children discover life through active participation; they investigate the world of society through a mental experiment, Scarfe's definition (6) of make believe.

Make believe may be called the magic of the mind which enables children to concentrate on isolated elements in their real or imagined worlds. As they wrestle with problems of work and play, they increase their powers of accurate observation, their sensitivity to implications, and their awareness of multiple causes. They develop the power to create as their understanding increases. When they encounter the world of literature, they are able to envision the many possibilities suggested by a description or an incident.

Make believe is, first of all, a source of hope—hope for a solution, for something better. It safely enables an integration of feelings, needs, and interests with subject matter. A child can handle situations with a combination of ease and exertion of effort, proceeding to new ideas as existing ideas are validated. A child who feels both safe and free will reveal personality and highly personal ideas to others.

Each make believe experience is characterized by a freshness, an involvement of the whole being in the discovery process which ensues.

Krishnamurti (5) stated that discovery is the beginning of creativeness and that without creativeness, do what we may, there can be no peace nor happiness in the world.

Let's explore the possibilities of make believe's contribution to individual education.

Make Believe makes possible the courage "to be" and the catalyst for "becoming." Readiness for effective response as Glen, an imaginary rabbit, crouched behind an imaginary fence eyeing Mr. McGregor's every move, waiting for the watchful eye to disappear, thus giving him the signal for safety to wriggle under the fence.

Make Believe helps a child move toward clear-cut communication, as increased awareness tends to bring everything into focus.

Make Believe reinforces the child's belief in the use of intuitive knowledge as the new experience requires coping.

Make Believe helps children gain insight into the "secret self." Karen, who had been afraid to respond, now admits, "I bet now I could be Mr. McGregor and scare 'em out, huh?"

Make Believe is a drawing-out process. If the child feels safe, initiation of new ideas follows.

Make Believe makes possible for the child to handle situations with ease but with caution of effort if called by the "inner line."

Make Believe is the proliferating product of creative spirit and intellectual vigor. Five year old Mark suggested, following the creation of the make believe garden by his friends, "Next time, let's build an electric fence—that will pull all the hair out of the rabbits!"

Make Believe makes possible the melding of emotion and intellect which Scarfe indicates is the true character of a complete education.

Make Believe makes it possible to practice handling freedom. The artistic teacher suggests subtly, setting limits: "Let's make a circle as round as something we see in this room. When you have helped make the circle round, let go of hands."

Make Believe points the way to self-discovery and self-realization. Bud's experience with The Rabbit who wanted Red Wings gave him a feeling of joy with the newly sprouted wings, but later helped him realize the new addition was of little value when no one recognized him, not even his mother.

Make Believe helps children to see what human beings are really like. Pretending to be mother, father, teacher, Pam next door, brings insight into how human beings relate and respond.

Make Believe opens "inspiration channels," helps a child to become more sensitive to impressions (especially beauty), puts the child at ease with verbalization. "Let's open the big grey cloud," suggested Sacha, "so that the saggy flower can lift its head."

Make Believe provides wide and deep channels for drawing out emotional forces, ultimately introducing cooperation and commitment to task. Paul wanted to be the man "who beat their brains in" in *The Tale of Peter Rabbit*. When the teacher asked for one who could frighten the rabbits out of the imaginary garden without beating their brains in, Paul was the first to volunteer a good alternative.

Make Believe helps remove unpleasant situations presented by those unable to control behavior without some guidance. "Let's find a place for rope turning that will not bump anybody" set limits within which Mike operated safely.

Make Believe makes possible the feeling of power that comes with self-control. "Those of you who can walk down the hall without bumping anybody may go." (Who will publicly admit it's impossible?)

Make Believe provides a rich source of satisfaction by being the cause of something which is ultimately, if not almost immediately, successful. Scott, as Peter Rabbit, moving into the imaginary garden, commented, "I couldn't hear my own feet!"

Make Believe creates techniques suitable for personal use. "Let me do it my way!" is often heard by the kindergarten teacher. Children-created techniques usually predict success rather than failure.

Make Believe helps young children face fearful situations. Sylvia, as Little Red Riding Hood, walks through the woods to Grandmother's house anticipating fearful events, but summons courage to cope with the make believe situation.

Make Believe makes possible the assumption of a role reserved for the child in the near future. Lisa had not yet had a polio shot, but through make believe experience saw what it was like, and was able to face the shot with a lessened degree of fear.

Make Believe occurs in a climate conducive to constructive creative expression, for revealing one's inner self is a highly personal affair and will happen only when a feeling of safety is prevalent.

Make Believe makes it possible to balance the world of work and play, and, according to Frye (2), demands that we continue to do both. As children work and play, he believes they develop the power to create and the power to understand with increased sensitivity, awareness, accuracy in observation, and improvement in taste and judgment. A vision of possibilities spreads before the child who makes believe and who sees other children do the same. Respect for self and for others is in full flower. As Crosby points out, what counts in the lives of children who are shaping their future and the future of their children is being able to live richly in the present.

MAKE BELIEVE ACTIVITIES

A community sponsored program, a cooperative venture in which parents and public libraries have supported the serious business of make believe, has provided delightful learning experiences for about 25 years. "Let's Pretend with the Fours and Fives," a program steeped in the magic of make believe, has involved over 3,000 participants yearly, placing emphasis on the carryover into everyday life of the following values absorbed through identification with storybook characters: confidence, curiosity, courage, humor, understanding, persistence, patience, honesty, loyalty, compassion, thoughtfulness, awareness, hope and commitment.

While evaluation is difficult, comments from former participants, many of them now college graduates, include:

"It was fun."
"I have never been afraid to try anything after being in the program for five years."
"I think I fell in love with books through the program."
"I had chances to practice being a better person."
"I am always curious about what's between the covers of books."
"I learned how to carry through something I started."
"I know I will see that my children have the program."
"I think I learned how to listen with my heart and that's the way I learn best and remember." (It is James Stephens who believes that the head does not hear anything until the heart has listened, and what the heart knows today, the head will understand tomorrow.)

A make believe activity for college students in storytelling classes resulted in the publication of real books without words. These students designed books of nursery rhymes which three year olds read with great success. As soon as they can recite a nursery rhyme, they can pick up *There Was a Crooked Man* and read each wordless page. One delightful comment from a young one after he put down *Humpty Dumpty,* "I can read, and I haven't even gone to school yet!"

Multisensory enrichment can enhance listening with the heart through the following suggestions:
- Take a walk, alone along the beach, through a forest, listen to the wind, look for signs of Spring, Winter, Summer, Fall.
- What is the most beautiful sight in the world? One student wrote:

    The world is so full of beautiful things
    Won't you take time to see?
    Lay aside every care and just for awhile
    Come take a walk with me.

    Have you seen the daisies with smiling faces
    Or the rainbow arched in the sky
    Have you seen a river flow joyously onward
    And the soft white clouds drift by?...

- Colors can call up imaginative experiences and imaginative expressions. What is your favorite color?
    One parent wrote:

    Black is the night sky turned onyx, shimmering bright
    It's peace, rest, quiet sleep when anxious moments take flight.

And it's terror, intrigue, and a bomb dropped at night.
Black is earth with bright gems hidden deep in its bed....
Black's refined, enigmatic, compelling, emphatic,
It's intriguing, strategic, accenting, ecstatic.
And when I wear black I feel refined and dramatic....

The principal's contribution:

White is the starchy crisp of fresh, clean sheets.
White is the color of cleanliness in a doctor's gown.
White is the color of the calling card of the executive.
White is the color of a fresh substitute in a muddy football game....

A fifth grade student wrote:

Pink is the color I like the best
If I were a bird, I'd put pink in my nest....

- Problems can activate imagination, promote clearcut, colorful communication and commitment to improvement or alleviate the problem while instilling a feeling of compassion. A group of fifth grade boys and girls was asked: If you could have a solution to your most pressing problem by the time school is out today, what would it be?
One wrote:

From the time I was born
My sister was there
And ever since then,
She's been in my hair.
"No! Not my socks
No! Not my shirts.
No! Not my ties.
And No! Not my skirts.
I long for the beads and bracelets
That older girls wear.
But if it weren't for my sister
I'd not be on top
For she is the one who
Taught me to "bop."

From the first family of another culture to move into the community, a third grade student wrote:

I was born.
My Mammy sang me a lullaby.
I didn't know that it mattered then
But soon I found that
Dirt looked different on my hands.

I grew.
"No work for you here," they said.
"No food for you."
I was born.
I wish I'd never heard that lullaby.

From a sixth grade boy who knew ahead of time that he would have to stay in after school on Wednesday:

My pencil is a funny thing.
It always feels like doodling.
It's funny that it doesn't say,
"Why don't you get your work done,
instead of play?"

- Picture words challenge the imagination, enriching the language experience.

FUN with WORDS

LOOK
do$ar
"COOL"
hot
ODOR
MOUNTAIN
SALMON
APPLE

- Dictionaries become worn, and minds become stretched when, for example, one thinks of as many words as possible to substitute for the word "move." Some of the 150 words which college students thought of:

glaze	build	flow	jimmy	ogle	nod
hoot	kick	flow	comb	shove	spin
bowl	call	bruise	bank	bite	animate
decide	hurry	shift	rock	xerox	sputter

- When parents and teachers use Walter de la Mare's criterion that only the rarest kind of best can be good enough for the young, they arrange to:

    1. Develop a capacity to care about what happens to children and adults.
    2. Create a restful room by being relaxed.

3. Allow "wonder" to permeate the classroom.
4. Be aware of, and develop appreciation for, change.
5. Help each child discover his or her gift.
6. Look upon the "new" as an adventure.
7. Develop a keen sensitivity to the minute, myriad changes in children.
8. "Fence in" the pasture of creativity.
9. Remove all barriers of race, color, creed, and sex in promoting a feeling of personal worth.
10. Keep space in the garden for "late bloomers."
11. Encourage and appreciate the imaginative expressions of children.
12. Develop responsibility by providing opportunities to become responsible.
13. Work toward goals, but be more interested in the growth that takes place than results which accrue.
14. Help each child evaluate results of actions and reactions.
15. Have fun!

Every parent and teacher possesses the magical power to provide the challenging experiences which children need to become happy productive citizens in a democracy. Moreover, learning acquired with the aid of imagination helps the child cope with unforeseen situations when confronting them in the real world. After all, to those who have faced new problems, thought about them and found a means for solving them, the process is familiar. The vicarious experiences in the world of imagination develops confidence, readiness and the ability to respond effectively to unexpected situations.

Through identification with human experiences which help build rather than destroy, the courage and confidence to go beyond that which is expected and the wisdom and ability to respond effectively to change develop on a high level through a dramatic process of thinking, feeling, experiencing—a process which affords the learner opportunity to achieve full self-realization in the world of tomorrow.

SUMMARY

Make believe—using imagination to create a way to handle a situation—enables the individual to practice various skills of creating and to acquire the ability to create in time of need. Suggestions for make believe for individual education include a variety of activities in which children enact scenes, recognize limits, acknowledge causes of success, experiment with techniques, verbalize impressions, view the efforts of others, repeat scenes with variations, assume various roles, experience emotions, act out real life scenes, and dramatize fairy tale characters.

It's all there, in the hearts and minds of children...free for the asking. When will we return a listening ear to those who communicate loud and clear?

References
1. Cane, Florence. *The Artist in Each of Us.* New York: Pantheon Books, 1951.
2. Frye, Northrop. *The Educated Imagination.* Bloomington, Indiana: Indiana University Press, 1964.
3. Holbrook, David. *English for the Rejected.* London: Cambridge University Press, 1964.
4. Isaacs, Susan. *The Nursery Years.* New York: Schocken Books, 1968.
5. Krishnamarti. *Seattle and King County Libraries Newsletter.* Seattle, Washington, 1953.
6. Scarfe, Neville. "Play in Education," unpublished lecture given at the University of British Columbia, 1950.
7. Woods, Margaret S. "Are You Creative or Computerized?" *Overview,* University of Washington Student Teacher Journal, 1972.
8. Woods, Margaret S. *Creative Dramatics in the Classroom.* Couperville, Washington: The Seven C's, 1984.
9. Woods, Margaret S. *Creativity: Process and Product.* Couperville, Washington: The Seven C's, 1984.
10. Woods, Margaret S. *Let's Take a Chance on Change.* Couperville, Washington: The Seven C's, 1984.
11. Woods, Margaret S. *Storied Ventures.* Couperville, Washington: The Seven C's, 1984.
12. Woods, Margaret S. *Thinking, Feeling, Experiencing: Toward Realization of Full Potential.* Couperville, Washington: The Seven C's, 1984.
13. Woods, Margaret S. *Wonderwork.* Couperville, Washington: The Seven C's.
14. Woods, Margaret S. *The Beauty and Logic of Creativity.* Couperville, Washington: The Seven C's, 1984.

CREATIVE READING CAN BE A BALANCE AND AN ANCHOR IN GUIDING THE GIFTED

Ann F. Isaacs
National Association for Gifted Children
Cincinnati, Ohio

It is a small wonder that the plight of the gifted child evokes little understanding or sympathy. Most parents do not know when their children are gifted, and teachers do not recognize the gifted in their classrooms. More than half of school administrators think there are no such children in their schools (20). Educational literature and psychology seldom mention the gifted child; when there is discussion, the difficulties of being gifted are rarely emphasized.

It should be apparent that conflicts may arise at some stage of the gifted child's interaction with others, simply because the child's expectations and/or responses will differ from those of other children and hence will not seem appropriate or normal in the situation. This chapter explores some of the problems and suggests procedures related to reading instruction that may reduce or eliminate conditions detrimental to gifted children.

SPECIAL NEEDS OF GIFTED CHILDREN

Possible Educational Problems

Some gifted children learn to read during their preschool years. A common fact, one rarely noted in the educational literature, is the tragic way these precocious learners fare. Instead of working in their favor, the advanced beginning can prove to be a negative achievement, since many teachers, although skilled in many ways, do not know how to cope with the five year old who reads.

Children who are able to read at the beginning of their first year of school may later show a decline rather than growth in reading. Thus, children who enter school reading unhaltingly may being to read falteringly. These children face a combination of negatives: A teacher whose attitudes may range from passivity to hostility, plus a peer group from whom they are often isolated. Consequently, punishment rather than reward is the reinforcement which early readers tend to receive.

Literature on the gifted may be misleading because it tends to stress achievements and fails to mention the gifted child's problems. Not uncommonly the gifted child needs remediation in reading. Many gifted children have been known to read several levels below their potential, a fact which would make average children candidates for remediation. When it is realized that the gifted should be able to read several levels above grade placement, their problems, when regarded in proper perspective, loom even larger than do the problems of average children (15).

Thus, many gifted children who should be receiving help remain unaided because their performance is acceptable when compared with the average. It is only when the underachievement is viewed within the range of what fellow gifted children with similar mental endowments are achieving that the true extent of these children's needs becomes apparent.

The beautiful part about helping the gifted child overcome a problem is that, with good rapport and constructive remediation, a teacher can be rapidly rewarded and find the time spent exceedingly worthwhile. With good achievement, the gifted child no longer requires additional time and effort from the teacher, and rapidly becomes an asset and aid to all classroom endeavors.

Some teachers take the attitude that parents of the gifted are too aggressive. Still others are ready to state that all parents think their children are gifted. These ideas are greatly in contrast to the facts, at least within my experience. More often the reverse is true; parents are highly hesitant about calling their children gifted and do so only with the greatest reluctance.

Many parents are more than willing to "explain away" a child's superiority. They will attribute achievement to the influence of an older sibling or to time spent with the child or to extra experience or to television. Teachers, too, are eagerly willing to suggest that any child could achieve similarly, given suitable opportunities.

It is unfortunate that nonachieving gifted children frequently are unidentified and neglected. These children experience personal suffering when functioning below potential because they sense that they should be performing at higher levels. This loss is ours as well, for if any one of us is diminished, we are all diminished. The greatest loss, of course, is that the far-reaching potential of the gifted child may never be realized.

Young parents who bring a gifted child to the first school experience need encouragement. Instead, they may be confronted with the first of a long series of battles as the child encounters new teachers. These boys and girls are so different from neighbor children that their precocious qualities may be evaluated negatively, rather than positively, with the child being ostracized from play with peers. At times, a parent has no way of knowing that his child's behavior is on a superior level. In some cases a majority of children in a given neighborhood may be gifted. The result may be that giftedness in such a situation is perceived as the norm, and again not properly valued.

The Needs of Gifted Early Readers

Durkin (5) found that early readers hold the gains they have made. She followed up the superior reader who arrived in school reading and found that, when compared six years later with other students of the same mental age, the superior ones had maintained their lead.

Isaacs (13) points out that early reading is not necessarily advisable for all gifted children. However, teachers must encourage children who do read at an early age and should:

1. Permit the child to read with children in higher grades.
2. Give the child opportunities to work with an outside consultant.
3. Enable the child to pursue other activities suggested by the consultant.
4. Excuse the child from routine library assignments.
5. Encourage other activities suggested by the librarian.
6. Permit the child to receive help from older students and to give help to younger students in other grades.
7. Encourage task-sharing with the child's own classmates.
8. Request other teachers to permit the child to share ideas with their classes.
9. Permit the child to help in the role of teacher's aide.
10. Arrange suitable grade placement, even if this requires skipping grades.
11. Promote writing of the child's own stories.
12. Allow time for dramatizing and directing the enactment of poems, stories, and plays.

It is a commonly held notion that most gifted children learn to read by themselves. (My experience suggests that, while most may be able to recognize words or phrases, only a very few are fluid independent readers.) Those who know gifted preschool children casually may believe that the children are reading fluidly and excellently. Frequently, however, what passes for reading is the love of books. Often the gifted child's superior memory appears to be reading. Close observation will reveal that the child is more often turning the pages and reciting from memory.

For gifted children, reading can be both balance and anchor. Reading gives perspective to their visions of who they are and who they might become. Reading opens up imaginary vistas which can, in maturity, become reality. The child whose environment is repeatedly circumscribed with limitations may find reading to be the magic carpet to the future and to the treasures of the world. A child's life at the moment may be impoverished, but the vast vistas to the future which reading opens can provide the proper springboard. To this child, the present becomes more acceptable in light of what the future may bring.

The Needs of Older Gifted Children

In contrast to popular opinion, many gifted children have reading problems. Careful diagnosis will reveal that they suffer some of the same emotional-psychological problems as do nongifted children. In addition, they have unique problems induced by their giftedness and attendant problems which may be characterized as psychosociological.

Teachers and principals sometimes mistakenly feel that helping gifted children regress to the norm is desirable, and they do their best to make this happen. It should be clear that children who first read several levels above grade placement, and then regress to grade level or below, are striving for social approval and are more eager to gain peer acceptance than to maintain their superior position as better readers.

Ability to excel is based on superior endowment and does not necessarily insure the development of efficient study skills (19). When parents and teachers discover deficiencies in a child's reading, problem sources need to be identified and eliminated.

In a conference, an eight year old boy (153 IQ on the revised LM Stanford-Binet Intelligence Scale) revealed how he and fellow classmates coped with boredom in the regular classroom. Although he was in the top reading group in his second grade, he confided that he had read the book they were using sixteen times. Was he then permitted to remain in his seat when his group was called? "Oh, no," he said. "Everyone has to go when the group is called except those who go to the bathroom."

"Do you mean those who *had* to go to the bathroom?"

"Well, some had to go. But others went to swing on the bars. Then, by the time they got back to the room, the reading group was half or two-thirds over."

(One wonders how the student knew this unless he too had been in the bathroom during his own reading-group time.)

WAYS TO GUIDE GIFTED CHILDREN IN AND THROUGH READING

Individualized Programs

Permitting a gifted child to choose his or her own books is a simple modification of individualized reading. This is the least difficult approach for the teacher and the one most appropriate for children who do not need the typical reading group. Books may be brought from home or selected from the library by the teacher or the child.

The individualized, personalized approach to reading has been successful when used by competent practitioners. Barbe (3), Witty (14), Duker (4), Spalding (18), and Williamson (21) are all in accord concerning the value of this mode of teaching reading. The children derive many benefits; they can:

1. Proceed at their own pace.
2. Develop a positive relationship with the teacher.
3. Experience success and improved self-esteem.
4. Be responsible for their own reading.
5. Have freedom in the selection of materials.
6. Discuss their reading with someone.

The advantages of individualized reading are many, the following being most important for gifted children and their teachers:

1. The program enables the teacher to meet the needs of each child.
2. Conferences and reports provide a means for diagnosis.
3. The teacher has time to spend with individual children at critical moments.
4. The teacher can provide a carefully structured program to develop skills.
5. The teacher attains a higher degree of job satisfaction.
6. The teacher becomes a director of learning.

Creative Reading Programs

Creative reading is the highest type and most neglected reading skill. Typically, reading is taught with "note the details and central thought" approach. The creative reader is capable of divergent responses rather than convergent ones. The creative reader possesses the ability to examine relationships among facts and interpretations.

The extent of children's interest in reading and the number of books they read may provide clues to giftedness. But without guidance, creative reading may never happen. Materials which are randomly selected, even when voraciously pursued, will not provide maximum benefits to a child. Reading rate and comprehension may grow, but the motivation for reading may remain at the escape level rather than proceed to the mature growth and insight level.

Books can transport the reader to imaginary ports. This purpose of stirring the imagination is not to be denied nor demeaned. Reading also contains the power of helping children realize who they are and, more importantly, who they can hope to become.

We can foster creative reading by making available all kinds of good books. Children are helped by having the opportunity to become more critical and more self-directing. They can be encouraged to demonstrate their reactions and interpretations through laughing, crying, and recounting, and even to change their language patterns through conscious effort (2).

Learning to read critically but constructively, and rewriting what does not appeal, can improve both critical and creative abilities. The same approach can be used to gain a higher order of involvement and application from the gifted as they are introduced to various forms of literature (6). This is in keeping with one of the goals of helping the gifted gain mastery of communication skills, enabling them to share their talents.

Self-acceptance can grow as a result of positive experiences and rewarding creative efforts. Underachievers have often been found to be self-rejecting, but they too can have opportunities to create. Pilon (17) suggests picture books as tools for building confidence in nonreaders.

Flexible Language Arts Programs

Flexibility in reading instruction for advanced students is an excellent mode of meeting individual needs (7). Progress is enhanced by good teaching, and fundamental skills still need to be given attention, sometimes at a faster pace. Learning prefixes, suffixes, and combining forms can increase vocabulary and materially aid both oral and written communication (12). Grade levels should not set the limits, and both classwork and individual assignments should be flexible. In addition, books, audiotapes, filmstrips, programmed learning materials, magazines, newspapers, and weekly scholastic papers are helpful. Gifted children are also especially fond of crossword puzzles, folk and fairy tales, science reading, and the Newbery and Caldecott award-winning books.

A sensitive teacher can provide practice opportunities for leadership and responsibility for the gifted. Simultaneously, the gifted child can be striving for further giftedness by gaining ability to give psychological comfort, being willing to teach others, and striving for high ideals and good judgment.

Both children and adults agree that sometimes the teacher can best serve a gifted student by leaving him or her alone. Gifted students do need, however, sources to which they may turn such as school personnel, the library, or lists of activities.

Bibliotherapy

Many gifted children, both contemporary and emeritus, have told me that they knew they were "different," but that they were never able to decide whether this difference was good or bad. A mature student in this field may conclude that the child suffered from a confused role-concept or faced an identity crisis. Although giftedness is ideally used for the good of all, it can be detrimental to society as well as painful to the individual. Helping a child understand giftedness is one of the most important roles an adult can fill, whether the child is already functioning at the gifted level or is not yet reaching an identified potential.

Teachers may find the works by Isaacs (*8, 9, 10, 11, 12, 14*) helpful. Articles in the *Gifted Child Quarterly* frequently focus on ways to encourage the gifted.

The writer has published a series which is useful to the teacher who has an occasional gifted child in class, or who wishes to assign readings to the whole class. The five articles in the series have several purposes. The intent is to describe some of the attributes of giftedness and to provide reinforcement through an annotated bibliography which emphasizes and exemplifies each of the traits. Another purpose of the series is to promote the older child's analysis of the writing styles and modes of achievement of objectives employed by each author. In a sense, the series might also be regarded as "minipreventive bibliotherapy." Children who might feel too different from others in the peer group could see themselves as not altogether unusual as they encounter people with diverse talents. Preventive bibliotherapy has been noted as helpful for these purposes: 1) providing vicarious experiences, 2) extending experiences, 3) building good mental health, 4) preventing and combating juvenile delinquency, 5) promoting developmental values, 6) forming character, 7) helping youth adjust to social and emotional situations, 8) furthering good human relations, and 9) providing a vehicle for personality growth. Reading lists can provide students materials which discuss the traits of gifted people and reinforce their development.

Enrichment Activities

The classroom teacher and the reading teacher should carefully select specific activities to meet individual gifted children's needs. The following tasks, many suggested by creative graduate students during past years, appear to be valuable:

1. Keep a diary describing memorable experiences.
2. Write original verse, using interesting forms of poetry such as the tanka or the Japanese Haiku and using pictures or observations from the classroom window as stimulation.
3. Write stories about different phases of growing up, such as "Important Happenings," "Important People in My Life," "My Library," and "The Most Exciting Event of My Life."
4. Make collections of myths, legends, mottoes, and proverbs.
5. Study the history of languages.
6. Use different materials, such as supplemental books on a topic, Landmark Books, Merrill Company Literature Series, encyclopedias, newspapers, book sections of Sunday newspapers, editorials, sets of supplemental science books, and magazines such as *Reader's Digest, National Geographic, Popular Science, Time,* and *Newsweek.*
7. Keep records for class activities: committee membership, lists of jobs to be done, materials to use.
8. If the class is going to be reading a story with a definite geographical locale or other specialized content, become a specialist on the subject ahead of time.
9. Read and discuss fine pieces of literature appropriate to interests and maturity levels.
10. Listen to excellent recordings to poetry and prose.
11. Chair a committee to discuss a good book which all have read.
12. Visit a lower grade and discuss a story to stimulate interest in reading.
13. Plan and build a personal library.
14. Catalog personal books.
15. Catalog the books in a classroom library.
16. Develop an up-to-date list related to a favorite hobby or interest.
17. Compile a bibliography of interesting books for the class to use for summer reading.
18. Arrange displays for book fairs, for parents, and for other classes in the school.
19. Implement a program for the school, such as costumed book parades, quiz shows, puppet shows, and/or character sketches.

20. Organize a junior "great books club," enabling several students to discuss a book that has been read by all.
21. Set up a book swap shop for either loans or trades.
22. Check reading rate; then use materials designed to improve rate, and chart progress.
23. Keep an individual account of materials read with notations.
24. Set up evaluative criteria, evaluate children's magazines, and make a recommended list for the library.
25. Compare the illustrations in different editions of fairy tales.
26. Report on the works and style of a favorite author.
27. Construct crossword puzzles using specific vocabulary.
28. Create and play language games which involve new words or words with multiple meanings, or games using the dictionary.
29. Compile a reading notebook containing excerpts which are unusually expressive.
30. View a television program; check facts presented in written materials with those given on the program.
31. Form a poetry club which enables members to discuss favorite poems, memorize well-know poems, or compose original poems.
32. Write dramatizations and stories of historical events.
33. Participate in all phases of theater production (directing, stage lighting, stagecraft, acting).
34. Read widely to select material suitable for plays, tableaus, monologues, and puppet shows; do research necessary for staging the production.
35. Make tape recordings of oral presentations to help in self-evaluation and improvement.
36. Interview an adult or pupil from an upper grade with specific questions in mind; organize the information to present to the class.
37. Create and stage a comic opera.
38. Direct and participate in creative dramatics and choral speaking.
39. Portray a character role in a monologue.
40. Tell a story through a sequence of pictures, pantomime, dance, tableaus, dramatizations, or choral speaking.
41. In presentations, use handicrafts such as puppetry, dioramas, stage settings, costumed dolls, shadow screen, or feltboard cutouts.
42. Select and prepare a story for sharing orally with another grade group or with the class.
43. Practice public speaking by giving two-minute impromptu speeches; keep a file of possible topics.
44. Discuss a children's theatre presentation; tell how the plot developed and analyze character development.
45. Explain with clarity a technical subject, such as a factory operation or some astronomical phenomenon.
46. Plan and give explicit directions for playing a game, making an object, organizing activities, or carrying out science experiments.
47. Read aloud various types of poetry, observing rules of poetic expression.

48. Give commentaries for silent movies, filmstrips, or slide showings.
49. Plan and present a play for a particular age group.
50. Learn to distinguish between statements of fact and opinion; by giving supporting evidence, prove that an article is based on one or the other.
51. Make a display showing examples of various propaganda techniques.
52. Compare getting information by listening to obtaining it from reading; compare the devices used in the two processes.
53. Analyze two talks on the same subject; try to determine why one was more interesting than the other.
54. Learn to take notes from reading or a lecture; learn to outline and to summarize.
55. Document research, using bibliographies, footnotes, and quotations.
56. Compile bibliographies for several topics or events, or about subjects of interest.
57. Constructively evaluate televised or school programs which the class has viewed.
58. make up and tell tall tales.
59. Tape record speeches and reports for class members to listen to individually.
60. Make oral or written reports of concerts, plays, and visits to museums.
61. Write book reviews and character sketches.
62. Write news stories, editorials, special columns, and advertisements for a school newspaper, a class newspaper, or a large wall-mounted newspaper.
63. Assemble and edit material for school or class newspapers, scrapbooks, or social studies units.
64. Write letters requesting materials for class use on units or topics being studied.
65. Take 5-10 minutes to write about anything, or to write about something (real or imaginary) that happened yesterday, or to describe something seen on the way to school.
66. Look at some objects (tree or landscape) until something is noted that was not seen before; write new impressions.
67. Express in writing feelings about music, paintings, or other art creations.
68. Write unfinished stories for another person to complete.
69. Write a story about a character from a favorite story.
70. Correspond with hospitalized veterans, particularly at holiday seasons.
71. Prepare scrapbooks of information and materials to exchange with children from other parts of the country or world.
72. Design unusual invitations to class parties or programs.
73. Write letters to imaginary friends about fictitious travels.
74. Imagine another period or place; write letters describing the setting.
75. Write an imaginary letter from one story character to another, telling something which happened after the story ended.
76. Write and illustrate stories, using local events, pictures, music, personal friends, or favorite story characters.
77. Conduct committee and class meetings.
78. Introduce guest speakers.
79. Use parliamentary procedures when suitable.

80. Write plays, poetry, descriptions, biographies, and autobiographies.
81. Convert a short story into a short play.
82. Create a poem about a painting seen in a book or a gallery.
83. Try writing a variety of story types and verse forms such as the fable, myth, parable, ode, ballad, limerick, riddle, or couplet.
84. Make a magazine for the classroom by compiling voluntary contributions.
85. Collect folklore, such as rope-jumping rhymes, counting-out rhymes, legends, and folk songs.
86. Make a collection of favorite poems.
87. Study the origin and derivation of words, names, places, persons, and flowers.
88. Create characters for a continuing story, adding episodes from time to time.
89. Write descriptions of unusual events, animals, and people; place these in a looseleaf notebook for sharing.
90. Participate in dramatic clubs, literary clubs, storytelling clubs, and book fairs.
91. Write an article persuading people to a point of view by using biased words and appropriate propaganda.
92. Write scripts for radio programs.
93. Participate in and produce radio and television programs.
94. Analyze an author's point of view in a particular book; read about the author in order to explain it.
95. Organize a file box for new words, arranging them under headings such as "Descriptive Words," "Words with More Than One Meaning," or "Additions to the Language."

SUMMARY

Gifted children frequently develop personal, social, or educational problems as a result of their divergent, creative behavior. While their needs at each stage of development are many, teachers are in a special position to provide an environment that will free these children to learn in terms of their own interests, styles, and rates. Through a carefully planned reading program—expanded to include all of the language arts areas—the teacher may guide gifted children toward the personal, social, and academic successes for which they have the potential.

For gifted children, adaptations of the regular classroom program must be made. There are benefits to be derived from individualized programs, linguistic study, creative reading programs, flexible language arts programs, and bibliotherapy. In addition, there are numerous special activities suitable for individual children.

References
1. Arnold, Lois V. "I'll Never Forget What's His Name," in Helen K. Smith (Ed.), *Meeting Individual Needs in Reading.* Newark, Delaware: International Reading Association, 1971, 133-144.

2. Bamman, Henry A. "Language Arts for the Academically Talented," in Helen K. Smith (Ed.), *Meeting Individual Needs in Reading.* Newark, Delaware: International Reading Association, 1971, 143-149.
3. Barbe, Walter B. *Educator's Guide to Personalized Reading Instruction.* Englewood Cliffs, New Jersey: Prentice-Hall, 1961.
4. Duker, Sam. *Individualized Reading: Readings.* Metuchen, New Jersey: Scarecrow Press, 1969.
5. Durkin, Dolores. *Children Who Read Early.* New York: Teachers College Press, Columbia University, 1966.
6. Ehrlich, Virginia A. *Teaching Literature to the Gifted.* New York: Board of Education, City of New York, 1970.
7. Furr, Oneta R. "Improving Flexibility in Reading for the Advanced Student," in Helen K. Smith (Ed.), *Meeting Individual Needs in Reading.* Newark, Delaware: International Reading Association, 1971, 124-132.
8. Isaacs, Ann F. "For Gifted Boys' and Girls' Personality Growth and Writing Skills," *Gifted Child Quarterly,* 12 (1968), 47-49.
9. Isaacs, Ann F. "Gifted Children Benefit from Learning to Be Self-Accepting," *Gifted Child Quarterly,* 12 (1968), 85-88.
10. Isaacs, Ann F. "Leadership and Ability to Accept Responsibility Are Among the Most Important Attributes of the Gifted," *Gifted Child Quarterly,* 12 (1968), 227-229.
11. Isaacs, Ann F. "Self-Sufficiency Is a Trait which Many Use in Describing the Gifted," *Gifted Child Quarterly,* 12 (1968) 181-182.
12. Isaacs, Ann F. "Vocabulary Enrichment for Which We Can Thank the Greeks," *Gifted Child Quarterly,* 15 (1971), 311-312.
13. Isaacs, Ann F. "Should the Gifted Preschool Child Be Taught to Read?" *Gifted Child Quarterly,* 5 (1963), 72-77.
14. Isaacs, Ann F. "Special for Boys and Girls and their Adults," *Gifted Child Quarterly,* 11 (1967), 252-253.
15. Krippner, Stanley, and C. Heald. "Reading Disabilities among the Academically Talented," *Gifted Child Quarterly,* 7 (1964), 12-20.
16. Marckwart, A.H. (Ed.). *Linguistics in School Programs.* Chicago: National Society for the Study of Education, 1970.
17. Pilon, A. Barbara. "Pick a Peck of Picture Books," *Gifted Child Quarterly,* 16 (1972), 11-17.
18. Spalding, Robert L. "Personalized Education in Southside Schools," *Elementary School Journal,* January 1970, 180-189.
19. Robinson, F.P. "Study Skills for Superior Students in Secondary Schools," in L.E. Hafner (Ed.), *Improving Reading in Secondary Schools.* New York: Macmillan, 1967, 175-180.
20. U.S. Office of Education, *Education of the Gifted and Talented.* Report to Congress by the U.S. Commissioner of Education and background papers submitted to the U.S. Office of Education. Washington, D.C.: U.S. Government Printing Office, 1972, (72-502 0).
21. Williamson, Ann. "Personalized Reading Progress—Multi-Aged Nongrading," in Helen K. Smith (Ed.), *Meeting Individual Needs in Reading.* Newark, Delaware: International Reading Association, 1971, 36-42.

FOSTERING CREATIVITY IN CHILDREN WHO DIFFER

Michael Labuda
Jersey City State College
and
Helen J. James
Houston, Texas

Children who are identified as gifted or creative are a unique population. They have in common characteristics which permit them to approach situations without preformed ideas; to produce unusual solutions to problems; and to view the world in ways that result in fresh, open-ended, or divergent consequences. On the other hand, creative children vary considerably in measured intelligence, aptitudes, and interests. As a total group, they are probably more different than they are alike, at least in ways that can be observed and measured.

During the past twelve years, gifted and creative children have been found among children who are classified as 1) minority group members or 2) learning disabled children. Such children are rarely categorized as gifted or creative and may be described in derogatory terms, such as "nonconforming" or "clever in nonacademic ways." That these children exist is a matter of record; that they exist and are not identified as gifted or creative calls attention to the high value given to academics. In another sense, the failure to identify these children points up our narrow, limited views of the child who "differs."

This chapter explores, albeit briefly and conservatively, the needs of children who, had they not been first classified as either culturally disadvantaged or learning disabled, could and should be members of the diverse group of gifted and creative children. Provisions for such children demand a special kind of teacher, yet one who might well be little different from the competent, ingenious teacher who attempts to meet the needs of all children.

NEEDS OF CHILDREN CLASSIFIED AS "MINORITY GROUP MEMBERS"

The Results of History

The views of Americans toward newcomers have fluctuated over the years. Initially, immigrants who spoke many different languages were assumed to enter the mainstream of a typical America and emerge as Americans, all essentially alike and all speaking standard American English. It would appear that other nations of the world had similar expectations of permanent settlers, or the expectation that large settling groups would assimilate native subgroups, the end result being a relatively homogeneous population.

In all instances where countless immigrants joined a populace in a melting-pot situation, the transformation was far more myth than fact. In many cases, a bicultural style developed, with various subgroups coexisting and influencing each other over a long period of time. As a result, nations of the world must now come to grips with the meaning of a multicultural society.

In a pluralistic society, minorities feel somewhat threatened by the dominant groups; thus, they move into closed ethnic circles. The develop ways of behaving that are acceptable, successful, and inclusive of the customs and language required within the closed group.

The child whose thoughts and language differ from the norms of an academic world cannot avoid confusion, failure, and personality disintegration if he or she is expected to conform to the norms of the new world. The culturally different child who possesses talents and demonstrates creative ways of coping with problems in a subculture seems to develop almost instantaneously a sensitivity or insight concerning school conditions that dictates the concealment of abilities. The child may adopt silence as a mode of response, or may become aggressive about things in general. The child may resist with surprising strength any attempt to elicit responses and, consequently, will be categorized as "culturally disadvantaged" and relegated to programs that are compensatory rather than enriching. Unless something occurs to reveal this giftedness, this child continues on a self-selected, obscure, and relatively safe course.

Types of Divergence

Some households within minority groups are not child-centered; that is, no adult normally takes time to play or to talk with the child. Children are expected to grow up as quickly as possible and to make their own way. They learn the quickest way to survive with a minimum of thought and conversation. However, a highly technological and achievement-oriented society requires complex thinking and language ability. To succeed, and the norm pushes for success, each individual's intellect must include the capacity for complex conceptualization. If possible, socialization should occur early to promote that complex development. Such conditions as poverty, limited perceptual experiences, and concrete modes of thinking and speaking greatly retard concept development.

Deprivations, whether economic or experiential, breed poverty of the intellect, leading to an inability to use educational and vocational opportunities, even when equitable social programs are available. Bruner and his associates (3) conclude that the research concerning symbolic intellectual development (i.e., language processes of all types) supports the hypothesis that culture influences modes of thinking and that the simpler the society, the less advancement the society expects of its children. Families from minority groups that have restricted verbal explicitness and use concrete, condensed meanings depend on extra verbal signals rather than symbols.

Bernstein (2) states that elaborated codes tend to be more universalistic and restricted codes, more particularistic. The implications for children from low socioeconomic groups is almost automatic failure in a school system which emphasizes middle-class standards, which tend to be more universalistic. Deutsch (6) notes that, because the culture of many minority groups is different from the culture that has molded the school and its educational theories and practices, children from minority groups come to school so poorly prepared that failure is inevitable.

The view of giftedness as a product of superior opportunity has led to a more careful examination of environmental factors. It has been demonstrated that improved economic status, hence greater opportunities, has increased the production of minority groups. In addition, such factors as family values and interaction patterns, child-rearing practices, and self-concepts have been found to affect the development of individual children. It may be said that a variance from the norm of many factors will create problems (4, 8).

In some minority groups, the male is supposed to be the dominant person; in other groups, the female assumes the dominant role. In one-parent families, there is bound to be a problem of identification as well as problems concerning passivity and dependency. There is often lack of communication between male and female; women are often lonely and isolated, consequently hostile. Discipline is frequently harsh and physical; getting caught for a violation of rules is a crime rather than a misdemeanor. The care of children is custodial; in many cases, any custodian is acceptable.

Strong peer group affiliations supply social and emotional release, as well as friends, for both sexes and for both the young and old. Mothers try to encourage upward mobility, whereas fathers more often discourage it. Families are not likely to provide suitable occupational role models for their children. Thus, a child aspiring to a higher level than the parents has to rely on an exceptional relative, on the school, on movies, or on television for information as to what it is like to go to college or to work in a chosen profession. Several writers believe that peer group influences take over very early in a child's life. It can be inferred that children learn early to tune out the examples and arguments of well-intentioned adults.

There are other kinds of divergent behavior found among minority groups: great skill with oral language but little skill with written language, almost indestructible loyalty within family groups, and philosophical leanings that verge on bigotry or fanaticism. Certainly, children from groups exhibiting those behaviors will not fit the norms of most schools.

The types of divergence which concern us most, regardless of other aspects of minority group children's behaviors, are those which reveal needs-meeting and/or problem-solving abilities indicative of unusual insight and unique thought. At times, the means by which a child plays a silent role, "acts out" feelings of hostility, or resists authority are so creative that the child's teacher and peers see a "very brilliant kid." In some instances, the handicraft products or the storytelling skills of a child give evidence of giftedness. Frequently, the nature of the child's questions suggests that his or her vision of possibilities exceeds the expectancies for the age group.

Those who seek unique children among minority groups in kindergarten and primary grade classrooms usually find them. Their uniqueness is revealed to a great extent in the nature of the products they create, not necessarily in the degree of perfection. Occasionally, however, a child reveals creativity by lengthy attention to a task, refusing to stop a project even for lunch after having worked all morning without having had breakfast or a snack. A few children reveal enormous cravings for activities that require active and thoughtful participation and specific results, demonstrating a tenacity and a thirst for understanding far beyond normal.

One must not forget these minority children may have combinations of divergence that seem almost incompatible in terms of traditional educational programs. To be gifted and to seek actively for knowledge, yet to lack expressive vocabulary and be ignorant of basic social behaviors, will cause conflict in the child at the same time that his or her behavior causes consternation to the teacher. Hence, we must identify *all* aspects of divergence within an individual child (*11*).

The Role of the School

To fulfill its obligation to culturally different children, the school must become sensitive to their unique needs. This sensitivity means recognizing, accepting, and interpreting cues from the learner; seeking further information to clarify cues; and adapting instruction to the cues. This process will strengthen the dignity of the individual at the same time that it enables the school to observe and document specific behaviors. In treating a child as an important and respectable individual—one with feelings, attitudes, and experiences that are worthy of some attention—we must recognize strengths first, with the inventory of deficits coming later.

Sensitivity leads to long-range diagnosis and planning. To know the child and to fit the program to his or her needs are imperative. The teacher must observe using checklists, inventories of various types, anecdotal records, skills assessments, and tentative statements of diagnosis. Then, the implementation of a suitable program requires extensive knowledge of various approaches and techniques as well as an attitude of willingness to adapt constantly to assure success. Most of all, the teacher must understand how to use a child's strengths in order to overcome weaknesses (*4*).

Fantini and Weinstein (*9*) challenge educators to meet the common needs of all children without sacrificing individuality or cultural diversity. They suggest three major areas.

1. *Teaching the basic skills and concepts needed to understand the world.* These "learning how to learn" skills include convergent and divergent thinking, problem solving, and other similar process skills.
2. *Focusing on each child's individual talents, interests, and innate abilities.* The content would come from the child rather than from the school, although the school would provide experiences to enlarge the child's interests.
3. *Using group interaction, participation, and inquiry activities devoted to affective learning.* Through this approach, children will acquire learning for career orientation, parenthood, citizenship, and self-development—all necessary for each individual in every culture and subculture and to the total society of a diverse population.

As a result of increased sensitivity, careful diagnosis, adaptation of instruction, and focus on the three areas just described, the school can meet the needs of all children to a greater extent. In addition, it should be possible to identify and to plan individualized instruction for children who give evidence of giftedness.

Ideally, the school will exemplify by its own diversity of approaches the fact that it respects divergence and uniqueness. On the other hand, it may be more important during initial stages of change to give attention to one aspect only: learning to observe children with thoroughness and zeal. Out of the observations should emerge data that will determine plans for instruction—plans for individual classrooms and plans for the entire school, with plans for gifted and creative children in both.

NEEDS OF LEARNING DISABLED CHILDREN

Intelligence Versus Learning Abilities

Some children whose measured intelligence is normal or superior fail to learn academic skills because of significant deficits in perception, conceptualization, or verbal/nonverbal expressive abilities. Lerner (11) summarizes the various types of problems and individual theories that eventually led to the following definition of learning disabilities formulated by the National Advisory Committee on Handicapped Children in 1968 (12):

> Children with special learning disabilities exhibit a disorder in one or more of the basic psychological processes involved in understanding or using spoken or written languages. These may be manifested in disorders of listening, thinking, talking, reading, writing, spelling or arithmetic. They include conditions which have been referred to as perceptual handicaps, brain injury, minimal brain dysfunction, dyslexia, developmental aphasia, etc. They do not include learning problems which are due primarily to visual, hearing, or motor handicaps, to mental retardation, emotional disturbance, or to environmental disadvantage.

The definition excludes children who fail to learn because of low intelligence, emotional deprivation, environmental deprivation, or physiological sensory handicaps. It includes, in essence, children of normal and superior intelligence who do not perform in school according to their potential despite what can be assumed to be an adequate instructional program. The definition implies careful diagnosis before labeling a child. The estimate of incidence of children with specific learning disabilities is 1 to 3 percent of the school population (12).

Some interesting facts appear in the literature concerning certain learning disabled children: During preschool years, these children exhibited extraordinary curiosity about their world; they demonstrated creativity and certain specific talents. Some were called "highly verbal," others were described as "scientifically inclined" or "talented in mathematical activities." Neither parents of such children nor their kindergarten teachers envisioned difficulties in academic learning. In past years, many teachers have delayed referring such children for diagnosis because they had evidence of good intellectual functioning in many respects, even if the children were failing to master basic skills of abstract symbolization. Notations on school records would suggest that "in a year or two" these children would settle down to academics and make good progress. That they did not make gains in achievement caused many anxieties among children, parents, and teachers. As a result, many children acquired either poor attitudes toward school or severe emotional disturbance.

While not all learning disabled children demonstrate creativity or unusual talent, many do. In fact, some make up for inadequacies in learning abilities by compensating in such an unusual fashion that they mask their problems for years. For example, a child who cannot learn to spell will produce illegible handwriting, at the same time discussing her ideas with clarity and excellent vocabulary; she is permitted to dictate or to tape her thoughts, receiving approval and commendation. Or a child with expressive language problems may draw intricate pictures with suitable labels, demonstrating superior talent of one type and receiving recognition for his giftedness in that area. Another child may have almost no reading ability, yet, by discussing ideas with others and listening to other children read, will demonstrate knowledge and process ideas rapidly, even knowing precisely where to find a certain fact on a given page.

Other learning disabled children reveal insights in particular areas, on particular topics, and/or in problem solving. When using their strengths in classroom projects, they produce results that their peers, their parents, and teachers view as outstanding. The value of their productions, especially to themselves, is confirmation of their abilities to learn; this confirmation is essential to the child who lacks a specific ability and may well be the greatest motivating factor in remediating the deficiency.

Intelligence, as measured by individual tests such as the Wechsler Intelligence Scale for Children and the Stanford-Binet Intelligence Scale, appears to be a critical indicator of potential for creativity in children with specific learning disabilities. Careful observation and extensive diagnosis will help the teacher discriminate between children and identify those with giftedness or creative ability.

The Educational Task

After a comprehensive evaluation has been made of a child's assets and deficits, it is possible to establish objectives for maximum development. To attain the objectives, the child may require the services of psychologists, neurologists, ophthalmologists, and pediatricians, as well as the classroom teacher, a learning disabilities teacher, and other members of the educational staff (10).

For learning disabled children who are gifted or creative, a major goal is correlation of efforts so that they may pursue interests without interruption while receiving appropriate remediation for the disability. In most instances, the classroom activities at the age or grade level will enable them to produce creatively, provided the adults directing selection of projects understand how to use their strengths and overcome weaknesses. The learning disabilities teacher can furnish diagnostic information and assist the classroom teacher in planning suitable activities.

As pointed out in preceding sections of this volume, it is essential that inspired children work on problems that challenge them, avoid boredom from innocuous lessons, and maintain their interest in learning. Obviously, a child who does not learn certain skills easily and must practice extensively to master those skills verges on boredom, disinterest, inferiority, and failure. Successes with individual and group projects related to his or her interests and talents will balance frustrations with remedial lessons and rekindle determination to learn needed skills.

No individual teacher can have the time to work alone with a learning disabled child on projects. Pairs of children, small groups, and resource persons can accomplish much under the teacher's guidance. Librarians, art, music, and physical education teachers can assist in many ways. These coordinated efforts will require sharing of diagnostic summaries and recommendations for instruction supplied by learning disabilities teachers and other specialists.

Lerner (11) suggests that a pupil be "...involved in both analysis of his problem and evaluation of his performance...[and] take an active role in designing lessons and choosing materials." This collaboration of pupil and teacher on a continuing basis builds the child's self-concept, provides evidence of progress, and interests the child in learning. When children feel that their interests are acknowledged as worthy, they can view themselves as what they are: complex, unique individuals with certain strengths and certain weaknesses, with successes and problems, valued for their talents and helped to overcome deficiencies.

CREATIVE TEACHING AND LEARNING FOR CHILDREN WHO DIFFER

Since minority group children and learning disabled children require adaptation of instruction in terms of their interests and needs, many educational procedures of individualization are suitable. Various aspects of creative teaching are suggested throughout this volume. The recommendations in this section apply to all gifted and creative learners but especially to children who differ in the ways we have discussed in this chapter.

Personalizing Instruction

The creative teacher seeks to make learning relevant by inviting children's active participation in planning and implementing activities in which they are interested. The teacher uses a knowledge of pupils' interests and needs to introduce the processes in the general curriculum; pupils select the content to be used in teaching the required skills.

This approach to instruction, intended to assure each child that personal interests will be met, requires the teacher to be grounded in the structure of knowledge rather than in a mass of facts. A command of this structure enables the teacher to adapt it for pupils and to relate it to their own reality. The results will be divergent, open-ended, and meaningful to each individual child.

The respect for children's uniqueness and the provision of interesting experiences combine to free children so that they express themselves in various ways. They appreciate not only their own products but also the products of others; they see value in diverseness, and they learn from it. Given encouragement, they develop new means of communication, whether by spoken language, pantomime, or artistic endeavor. Eventually, they gain a clearer awareness of themselves and the world in which they live.

The child who is culturally different begins to move into reading and writing in a natural way, for this child develops a need to obtain information and a willingess to learn the skills. In working with other children who have academic skills, the child gains a conviction that he or she can learn the skills as well as others. If instruction is adapted to suit his or her learning style and rate, the child gradually becomes a reader, a writer, and a speller, and then can release creativity in additional ways.

While learning disabled children may not need the motivation to want to learn academic skills, they do need to involve themselves in academic tasks, if only vicariously, partly because they may absorb some elements of skills learning but mostly because this will make them members of the in-group achieving a goal. Often, these children will be able to suggest the creative touch to a project or to carry out a particular segment for which they possess the needed abilities. Their interests find fulfillment, and they maintain the momentum needed to sustain them during the period of remediation.

Attempting to verbalize without specific examples limits the meaning of individualizing or personalizing. The next part of this section supplies samples of creative behavior.

Imaginative Results

Real satisfaction in learning comes from the joy of creation and the solving of a problem or transforming an idea into reality. It also comes from activities which are interesting and worthy of a child's attention and concern and within his or her range of maturity.

An intermediate grade disadvantaged group from an urban setting were encouraged to draw upon their repertoire of experiences as they became concerned with the problem of pollution besetting society. They expressed their feelings and arranged their ideas in a pattern that was different from any previous pattern in their thinking; they wrote the following:

Pollution

People, people, what do you see?
I see pollution enveloping me.
Pollution, pollution, what do you see?
I see people making money off of me.
Money, money, what do you see?
I see industry loving me.
Industry, industry, what do you see?
I see fish dying because of me.
Fish, fish, what do you see?
I see animals joining me.

A creative fourth grade child from another urban disadvantaged setting was encouraged to experiment with ideas. She freely associated humor in her imaginings and related seemingly impossible situations.

The Gooma Looma Binta Boo

This strange creature is found in lakes and streams. He is a playful animal, but is known for his raging temper when tickled.

One reason the Gooma Looma Binta Boo is strange is because he has two heads, one arm, and six pink and yellow legs. He eats rocks, pebbles, and any kind of hard tasty food that he can munch on. I recommend him for a pet because he is friendly and loves children. I know; he just had my kid brother for lunch!

An eighth grade disadvantaged girl from Philadelphia always resisted but never with any determined show of will or anger. She was labeled by her teachers as a nonperformer. In a playful, yet purposeful, behavior, she sought a solution to saving the few trees found in cities by writing this:

A Day in the Life of a Tree

"It's great to get those nasty leaves off of me. They were bothering me all summer. Now I can relax....Oh, no! As we say in IOT (International Organization of Trees)." SLIT. "It's a slitter, dreadful enemy of me, a tree. Oh, that horrible carving knife. No initials, please!" SLIT. "Oh, pain, pain, pain!" SLIT! SLIT! SLIT! "Oh, stop, please stop! There's an R penetrating my twentieth ring, an M on my twenty-second, and an N slaughtering my eighteenth. RMN. Who could that be?? IOT will get him!"

As illustrated by these examples, children labeled as failures can meet with considerable success in their attempts to reveal their insights into situations. Hearing good literature, discussing ideas in an open environment, and having freedom to manipulate language to suit their fancies can elicit unique productions.

The ways in which learning disabled children communicate when they cannot spell and write frequently surprise teachers. A third grade girl was absolutely undaunted by the class assignment to write a personal letter. She rapidly drew a series of rough sketches to communicate a series of thoughts, then added "Dear" followed by a smiling face to the beginning and "Love" and her initials at the end. Asked to read her letter, she clearly stated a sentence for each sketch. Her letter was admired by her classmates, and she glowed with satisfaction.

Letter writing seems to have a special appeal to young children and may be a means of accomplishing reading goals in unexpected ways. One second grade boy who was unable to sit still for reading activities proceeded to learn many words as he spent much of each day writing letters to the teacher, his classmates, and visitors to the classroom. Apparently, the motor activity of writing allowed him to meet his need to move. Having to find out how to spell the words he needed allowed him interaction with other children, and writing the words impressed them on his memory so that he gained a good reading and spelling vocabulary.

He began to identify words in reading materials, and even if he had to walk around while doing his reading, he began to spend time reading to himself and to anyone who would listen.

An unusually creative six year old innercity boy surprised school personnel by drawing complicated pictures and dictating stories of over one hundred words within a few weeks after he entered school. He was happy to have his picture and story mounted; he would point out his story, but he would never sit to have it read to him nor try to identify any word in it. He taped stories and constructed his own setting and characters to dramatize the tales. He learned number facts, but he did not write them. After five months, his teacher bargained with him to get five minutes' effort in readiness activities leading to writing for each thirty minutes he had for his special projects. It became apparent that he was an expert judge of his disability, for his early writing revealed reversals, rotations, omissions, and substitutions. However, he made slow and genuine progress in recognizing letters and forming them. Gradually, he began to label his own pictures. He did not become a member of a reading group until the sixth month of second grade, when he suddenly seemed to have confidence in his ability to cope with what he called "a bunch of words." The individualized program had prevented failure and encouraged his efforts.

It may be that learning problems will not develop if teachers view children as unique in their rate, style, and pattern of learning and allow them to choose their own values and interests. Drew (7) states:

> By honoring these directions of growth and allowing them to flourish naturally, we found that students could master what had been difficult topics and materials and do this easily. As we have seen, a nonreader began to read without the pressure of applied methods and scheduled class periods. Students who habitually failed English found they could speak fluently and well when they could talk about something of interest rather than on an assigned topic. Just as the school came to a close, a boy who had been an indifferent mathematics student did four months' work in three days and ended up six weeks ahead of his classmates.

SUMMARY

Minority group children and learning disabled children are sometimes gifted or creative, although they are not first recognized as talented because their academic failures obscure whatever creativity they may demonstrate. Special attention that involves thorough diagnosis and individualized instruction may permit such children to live up to their creative potential as well as master needed basic skills.

Children from minority groups have divergent language, conceptualization abilities, and/or life styles that cause failure when they enter the traditional school setting. Yet some of these children reveal problem-solving abilities or needs meeting talents indicative of unusual insight and unique thought. The school must provide the means for good observation, diagnosis, and adaptation of instruction to prevent failure and to encourage these children in following their interests.

Learning disabled children have normal or superior intelligence accompanied by a specific deficit in perception, conceptualization, or receptive or expressive language abilities. Some of these children are extremely creative in compensating for a deficiency; others are particularly talented in one area of learning, such as mathematics or science. The educational task is twofold: The child's strengths must be used in challenging, rewarding ways; weaknesses must be overcome through expert remediation.

Personalized instruction will promote the learning of processes required in the general curriculum, at the same time assuring children that their personal interests are valuable and will be met. Both minority group children and learning disabled children will creat unique products as teachers adapt their instruction to meet specific needs of children. The results of their creative endeavors will be diverse, ranging from imaginative writing to handicraft and art.

References
1. Bernal, Ernest M. "The Education of the Culturally Different Gifted," in A. H. Passow (Ed.), *The Gifted and the Talented: Their Education and Development.* Seventy-Eighth Yearbook of the National Society for the Study of Education. Chicago: University of Chicago Press, 1979.
2. Bernstein, Basil. "Social Class and Linguistic Development: A Theory of Social Learning," in A. H. Halsey, J. Floud, and C. A. Anderson (Eds.), *Education, Economy, and Society.* New York: Free Press of Glencoe, 1961.
3. Bruner, Jerome S. et al. *Studies in Cognitive Growth.* New York: John Wiley and Sons, 1966.
4. Clark, Barbara. *Growing Up Gifted.* Columbus, Ohio: Charles E. Merrill, 1979.
5. Cooke, Gwendolyn J., and Alexinia Y. Baldwin. "Unique Needs of a Special Population," in A. H. Passow (Ed.), *The Gifted and the Talented: Their Education and Development.* Part 1. Seventy-Eight Yearbook of the National Society of the Study of Education. Chicago: University of Chicago Press, 1979.
6. Deutsch, Martin. "The Disadvantaged Child and the Learning Process," in A. H. Passow (Ed.), *Education in Depressed Areas.* New York: Teachers College Press, Columbia University, 1963.
7. Drews, Elizabeth Monroe. *Learning Together: How to Foster Creativity, Self-Fulfillment, and Social Awareness in Today's Students and Teachers.* Englewood Cliffs, New Jersey: Prentice-Hall, 1972.

8. *Education of the Gifted and Talented.* Report to Congress by the U.S. Commissioner of Education. Washington, D.C.: U.S. Government Printing Office, 1972. (72-502 0)
9. Fantini, Mario, and Gerald Weinstein. *The Disadvantaged.* New York: Holt, Rinehart and Winston, 1968.
10. Johnson, Doris J., and Helmer R. Myklebust. *Learning Disabilities: Educational Principles and Practices.* New York: Grune and Stratton, 1967.
11. Lerner, Janet. *Children with Learning Disabilities: Theories, Diagnosis, and Teaching Strategies.* Boston: Houghton Mifflin, 1971, 76.
12. National Advisory Committee on Handicapped Children. *Special Education for Handicapped Children.* First Annual Report. Washington, D.C.: U.S. Department of Health, Education, and Welfare, 1968.
13. Torrance, E. Paul. "Creatively Gifted and Disadvantaged Gifted Students," In Julian C. Stanley et. al (Eds.). *The Gifted and the Creative: A Fifty Year Perspective.* Baltimore, Maryland: Johns Hopkins University Press, 1977.

PART SIX
A LOOK AHEAD

Implementing change requires a serious examination of our philosophy and a clarification of problems and recommendations for meeting the individual needs of the gifted and creative as we foster reading growth. This brief glimpse of encouraging trends coupled with recommendations for an open, flexible, creative atmosphere provides a ray of light into the future. The present needs of the gifted and the creative have reached the crisis stage. Carefully planned provisions are needed. The individual, the school, and all concerned will be stimulated to undertake widespread efforts on behalf of the gifted and creative student. By extending and enriching significant contributions in the area of creative reading we will assure the leadership we want and need as we move into the 2000s.

ML

FORGING AHEAD IN READING FOR GIFTED AND CREATIVE LEARNERS

Michael Labuda
Jersey City State College

Interest in education of the gifted and creative has been somewhat cyclical, moving back and forth like a scale whose educational balance moves to or from the pursuits of excellence. However, some programs have operated continuously over long periods of time. Interest revived in education of gifted and creative in 1969 when Congress passed an addition to the Elementary and Secondary Education Amendment clarifying its support of financial benefits for the special educational needs of the gifted population. In addition, this act mandated a study to determine the extent to which needs were being met, how federal support can be more effective, and recommendations for new programs. This report (cited in Chapter 1), confirmed the impression of inadequate provisions for gifted and creative learners and the widespread misunderstanding about their needs.

The 70s was a banner decade for gifted and creative. The American public recognized the need for specialized education for the gifted and creative. National, state, and local educators, in cooperation with concerned parents, banded together in long range comprehensive planning to rectify some of the major problems. An Office of Gifted and Talented was established; all states identified personnel responsible for gifted education; national and local leaders emerged; Congress increased appropriations; state and local communities increased funding; model programs were funded; leadership training and university programs multiplied; teachers, materials, and program development increased due to federal and state reimbursements.

CURRENT TRENDS

One of the most encouraging trends developing out of the 70s movement was the emphasis on humanism. Rigid authoritarianism and its presence in the classroom was criticized by Holt, Kohl, Kozol, Postman, and others. Question asking became valued. Students began making observations, formulating definitions and performing intellectual operations that go beyond what someone else said was true. They developed an understanding of the skills necessary for understanding themselves and the dynamics of interaction with others as responsible, problem solving, intelligent citizens. This kind of instruction, whether formal or game play, provided the gifted with tools for analogy, problem solving, finding additional information, and making valid decisions.

Another result has been an openness in education that encourages tomorrow's minds (rather than attempting to reproduce yesterday's minds). Children are free to focus on unsolved parts of the curriculum rather than on the solved parts. Learning experiences are moving beyond memorization and simple cognition toward the advanced skill of interpreting in one's own words a new synthesis of ideas. Children's purposes form one focal point in the goals of the classroom. This instructional role serves as a basic ingredient for the production of reading materials assuring personal meaning for students as they read a wide variety of books at their own rate. Personal meaning for students becomes a basic ingredient in the instructional role. A wide variety of books and other informational and aesthetic sources has become available. With this freedom, learners develop their own dimensions of learning fully and creatively. In this type of environment they have a better chance to meet their needs without fear of rejection.

Another value deriving from this accessible, more efficient, and more rewarding environment is that a greater number of gifted students are assuming responsibilities in self-government and citizenry education programs. Trained personnel and community leaders are guiding the gifted in career exploration of known, unknown, and yet to be developed fields. Gifted students are also taking an active role in the learning situation. Enriched opportunities that provide stimulating experiences among various ethnic and racial minorities and children of the poor have been noted and have revealed exciting progress.

In developing higher levels of literacy, in the cognitive and affective domains, students attend aesthetic education programs and view professional performances at well known performing arts centers, advanced classes in mathematics, biology, and chemistry, university architecture courses, audio visual workshops, and a variety of talent classes.

Good programs for the gifted and creative have been reported in many books and journals, and these programs stand as examples of the best that education can presently offer. We build upon past successes as we innovate to meet our particular needs. Dedicated teachers are recognizing individual differences and are personalizing instruction to satisfy varied interests and needs of gifted and creative children. Personalized instruction is being streamlined according to how an individual learns and in what environment. Research indicates brains grow in spurts, and so curricula are being tailored to match stages of brain development. Torrance (5), Hatcher (1), Herrmann (2), and other researchers have suggested modifying curriculum to balance right and left hemisphere functions in order to encourage students' creativity. Synectics, multisensory and experiential learning, and creative thinking methods are being employed successfully. Students using both sides of the brain are using language and words creatively as they solve problems more readily and read faster and more efficiently. Teachers are basing instruction on how a particular student works best, and in what environment. Some instruction is aural, visual and kinesthetic in individualized, small group, or seminar type settings.

Striving to be truly accountable, more teachers are seeking to evaluate all children on the basis of their potential rather than on their status in the group. They realize that much available material can be adapted to meet the reading needs of gifted and creative learners. Teachers want to strike the initial spark of interest; they want to provide creative and imaginative experiences for their students. Consequently, demands are increasing for creative workshops and inservice courses, and teachers are learning a variety of techniques to stimulate children's thinking. Eagerness of teachers to stimulate gifted and creative students is producing originality and renewed interest in learning.

Although programs are inadequate to accommodate all the gifted and creative, it is encouraging to see a broader concept of giftedness which includes a capacity for high level creative responses. Schools must continue, extend, and more fully develop existing programs; other schools must identify and encourage creative learners by initiating substantial programs for the gifted.

Parents are actively involved in influencing local boards, state departments of education, and legislators to establish programs and bring about change in existing patterns for serving the gifted. Most parent efforts are in the home and overseeing local program development. Grotberg in an earlier chapter cited a variety of ways for parents to be involved in the education of their children. Parents as the first educators of their gifted children are nurturing their potential by fostering various viewpoints, reading to them, selecting quality reading materials, encouraging a depth of knowledge and perseverance, and inspiring pursuits that are fun.

Parents are working as partners with educators on curriculum study committees, publishing informational newsletters, lending support, and acting as a persuasive force in the community for supplementary funding. In some areas they are sponsoring enrichment classes outside of the school. United national, state, and local support has been helpful in obtaining the appointment of personnel responsible for gifted education programs in all state departments of education.

A LOOK AHEAD

The growing commitment in the concern and development of the gifted and creative suggests a bright future. The United States and Japan vying to produce scientists and breakthroughs in computer technology stimulated interest in improving both the quantity and quality of levels of learning.

In the 80s, the U.S. Office of Gifted and Talented was closed, and separate funding for the gifted was eliminated by the federal government for economic recovery reasons. This resulted in additional cuts by state and local governments.

Out of this dismal picture came a light of hope. A rekindled public and political awareness is emerging that is reversing the trend of Federal apathy. *A Nation at Risk* (3) and other studies have cited the importance of continued support of gifted and creative programs. Legislators, governors, and local educators, in cooperation with concerned parents, are supporting quality of life as a priority and indicated a willingness to support increased aid for gifted and creative programs. Senators Dodd (Connecticut), and Bradley (New Jersey) have cosponsored a bill to reinstitute the U.S. Office of Gifted and Talented within the Department of Education and authorize spending of $50 million annually. Congressman Murphy (Pennsylvania) proposed funding under this Education for Gifted and Talented Children and Youth Improvement Act of 1984. The bill will define the characteristics of gifted and talented and require the Secretary of Education to report to the Congress and public on the state of gifted education.

Education has become a lifelong pursuit. Electronic communications have opened doors for education at home, on the job, in a hospital bed, in the car, as well as in traditional classrooms. Individualized computer instruction is being used by people of all ages to gain new knowledge in basic skills, or to prepare for a second career. Life expectancy continues to increase and it is common for people to remain productive throughout their lives. Gifted electronic experts across the country are programming materials and creating classrooms using televisions, computers, and videotapes for libraries, museums, neighborhood centers, homes, and schools.

Although the workforce needs of the U.S. are not the same today as they will be in the future, schools will not disappear. However, students will control more of their learning. Reading will remain a prerequisite for successful living in our society. A wide range of teaching practices will be possible. These must, of course, go beyond the textbook type of learning situations prevalent today. The gifted and creative need individually suited and interesting reading experiences from the time they enter school. Therefore, the teacher will focus on higher thinking skills and reasoning and use reading throughout the entire day to encourage children to experience, think, and learn from varied, challenging, and appealing sources. Their students will focus on research, using their personal computers which they carry in their book bags. Within minutes they will retrieve information needed for reference work. Experience with different media will bring excitement as they develop skills and positive attitudes too often absent in today's learning process. In this integrated language arts curriculum, students will listen, discuss, read, and write as they immerse themselves in the total curriculum with reading becoming an interactive process for finding and creating materials. In the creative domains the gifted and talented will require the human catalyst—the teacher—for optimum development and achievement. All these experiences in reading must correlate with activities in creative writing and self-expression in multiple media, since children learn to read and refine skills in many ways. In areas such as creative writing, where there are many different right answers, machines will never teach as effectively as teachers.

As we prepare for the future we must promote teaching practices that aim at helping students become active readers. We want our students to ask questions, make predictions, to apply imagery, draw inferences, summarize, and elaborate as part of comprehending in an integrated language arts system. Through metacognition, students may learn to control effective reading strategies spontaneously and to monitor their own reading performance. We must include activities that include higher levels of thought, such as application, analysis, synthesis, and evaluation. Additions to the curriculum should include critical reading, creative reading, vocabulary development, wide exposure to literature, and productive thinking. For the gifted in language, school must extend language skills, guiding gifted and creative students to discover and use more sophisticated ideas and language patterns. In addition, assignments of diverse literary forms and styles of writing can flow naturally out of previous readings.

We cannot become complacent after observing encouraging signs of progress. We are far from the target of providing maximum development of all children in accordance with their unique nature and needs.

References
1. Hatcher, Margaret. "Whole Brain Learning," *School Administrator,* 40 (June 1983). (EJ285272 EA16603)
2. Herrmann, Ned. "The Creative Brain," *NASSP Bulletin,* 66 (September 1982). (EJ268225 EA 15606)
3. National Commission on Excellence in Education. *A Nation at Risk.* Washington, D.C.: U.S. Government Printing Office, 1983.
4. Passow, A Harry. (Ed.). *The Gifted and the Talented: Their Education and Development.* Seventy-eight Yearbook of the National Society for the Study of Education, Part I. Chicago: University of Chicago Press, 1979.
5. Torrance, E. Paul. "Hemisphericity and Creative Functioning," *Journal of Research and Development in Education,* 15 (Spring 1982). (EJ262568 SP511764)

THE TWENTY-FIRST CENTURY

Michael Labuda
Jersey City State College

As the technology of communications expands, people will be free to live where they want to rather than where their jobs are located. Employers and employees will be linked by satellites to a network of powerful computers that will permit people to work at home and have access to central records stored in business computers. We will be a civilization of total recall. Stored information will be both extensive and accurate. Communication will be by voice, electronic design, and reports. The result will be less drudgery and greater levels of productivity.

Computers will be many times more powerful than models in use today and linked to a vast communications network. In "Science City," Tsukuba, Japan, researchers have developed a Josephson element that will enable computers to process information ten times faster than those made with conventional silicon elements (3). Instead of tapping out instructions on a keyboard using esoteric language, people will use voice commands. Computers will store; speak; listen, recognize voices; translate into other languages; type and proofread messages to be sent or stored; receive, duplicate, and distribute appropriate materials to electronic mailboxes; make phone calls and appointments, and do endless mundane tasks (2, 4). Linked to banks, stores, government offices, and neighbors' homes, computers will reshape business from production to retailing, the very nature of work, and even the structure of the family.

Workers will be free to do creative assignments. Employees will be valued for their ability to synthesize, analyze, and hypothesize information and its application. Occupations available to computer enthusiasts will include computer aid designers, software writers, data processors, marketing, sales, finance and investment brokers, aerospace, computer maintenance, insurance, social sciences, engineers, technicians, and government.

Advanced automation, electronics, and computers will change our lives considerably. Business will be conducted in the home by teleconferences. Even now, more than half of the advanced manufacturing sector could be organized with low cost telecommunications and other equipment to allow people to work at home. Working at home permits flexible hours and avoids distractions. One will only need to meet with peers, colleagues, and superiors periodically to talk over problems.

When travel is necessary, cars using sensors and high speed microprocessors will automatically steer vehicles to and from destinations, trains will levitate above magnetically charged rails at high speeds, and planes will travel at supersonic speed. Computerized robots will perform most tasks, and production will be monitored directly from corporate headquarters to robots.

We will continue to manufacture key goods, but will need fewer workers to do so. At least 7,000 robots are at work in U.S. factories today. As their operation becomes more sophisticated, they will number in the millions. In a laboratory at "Science City," a computer controlled, multi-jointed, three finger manipulator robot has been developed that can hold articles and tie knots as skillfully as human beings (3).

Major scientific advances will enhance the production of land, water, and raw materials around the world. We are already in an era of quantum electronics, information theory, molecular biology, oceanics, nucleonics, ecology and space sciences.

Scientifically based energy systems offer many possibilities for the future. Possibilities range from photovoltaic cells that convert sunlight into electricity, tapping the heat of the earth itself, to using ocean wave power. Food production from farms, rain forests, and oceans will increase. New plant strains will grow in salty ground, bloom yearly without being planted, and be harvested up to three times each year. Fish will be cultivated by the millions in pond aquariums, and floating cities in the oceans will retrieve fish and plant life from the biosphere. The ocean floors also offer an array of minerals. Advances will be made in medical technology, earthquake forecasting, genetic engineering, artificial intelligence, weather modification, and health care.

Industrial opportunities will be available for robot designers and engineers, program monitoring and repairing of robots, transportation engineers, energy development and conservation engineers, electronic and computer engineers, genetic research, biomedical engineers, geriatric workers, agricultural economy, macroengineering, laser processing, bionic implant, managerial personnel, organization designers, and economists. In addition, business opportunities will continue in finance, insurance, trade, construction, manufacturing, transportation, utilities, services, and government.

Space shuttles will be used to manufacture exotic materials, put up communications satellites, and survey the globe for potential resources. Permanently staffed spacelabs will house scientists, researchers, analysts, and other space workers. The moon and nearby planets will be exploited for minerals that can be used in space construction. Many high technology materials require delicate, controlled handling, and the force of gravity can be a nuisance. In space, rare enzymes can be easily separated from cells, and laser and fiber optics materials can be manufactured without difficulty. It is estimated that there are at least four hundred different alloys that we cannot manufacture on earth because of gravity. As large space habitats are developed that provide comfortable quarters, grow their own food, and can exist independently of Earth, large-scale manufacturing plants and space tours will become common.

In addition to opportunities in the aerospace industry, there will be a need for creative thinkers and imaginative synthesizers as chemists, physicists, biologists, engineers, scientists, and high technology executives. All types of industrial and services personnel will be needed.

In the home and school, people will use voice computers and holography with advanced laser techniques, and the range of sound available in musical instruments will be expanded. Within seconds it will be possible to create a three dimensional image on the walls of a media room. Language will be dominated by visual images and mood altering colors rather than by words and sentences. Students will be able to observe the Royal Shakespeare Company performance of "Hamlet" on a 3-D stage.

More learning will occur outside the classroom. Children will grow up faster, display responsibility earlier, be more adaptable, and manifest greater individuality. Emphasis will be placed on studying the structure of everyday life, learning to allocate time, the personal uses of money, and places to go for help to solve complex problems in an ever-changing society. However, in addition to creating a balance in students' lives, schools will provide opportunities for developing reading abilities and applying them widely. A stimulating environment will create students who are inquisitive, exploratory, imaginative, and have adopted a problem solving approach to life.

The emphasis on affective education and the development of creative and productive thinkers who will be able to solve problems in new and effective ways will be extremely essential. As opportunities for learning expand, focus must be on reasoning, abstract thinking, formal operational thought, creativity, and knowledge in the basic subjects such as mathematics, chemistry, physics, and English. We must not leave the future to unfold by itself. Imaginative, flexible, and unthreatened educators can train today's students to address tomorrow's critical issues. Indeed, the future affects the present!

SUMMARY

The educational failure of the gifted and creative is not a problem limited to the school and the individual. If these children are to receive rewarding and beneficial experiences which contribute toward their growth, all parties involved—children, parents, administrators, teachers, and schools—must unite to provide the depth and breadth these neglected children so direly need to become the sophisticated and well-trained leaders of the future. The future world will be drastically different in many respects from the present world. Will our gifted and creative receive the training they need to continue to move our world forward?

References
1. Cogan, John C. "Should the U.S. Mimic Japanese Education?" *Phi Delta Kappan,* 65 (March 1984).
2. Toffler, Alvin. *The Third Wave.* New York: William Morrow, 1980.
3. *U.S. News and World Report.* "Science City: Japan's New Challenge to U.S," 94 (January 10, 1983).
4. *U.S. News and World Report.* "What the Next 50 Years Will Bring," 94 (May 9, 1983).

ORGANIZATIONS FOR THE GIFTED

American Association for Gifted
15 Gramercy Park
New York, New York, 10003

American Mensa, Limited
1701 West Third Street
Brooklyn, New York 11223

Association for Gifted
Council for Exceptional Children
1920 Association Drive
Reston, Virginia 22091

Gifted Students Institute for Research and Development
611 Ryan Plaza Drive, Suite 1149
Arlington, Texas 76011

International Reading Association
Special Interest Group on Gifted and Creative Students in Reading
CleoBell Heiple, Chairperson
1615 Second Avenue North
Upland, California 91786

National Association for Creative Children and Adults
8080 Spring Valley Drive
Cincinnati, Ohio 45236

National Association for Gifted Children
217 Gregory Drive
Hot Springs, Arkansas 71901

National Association for Gifted Children
World Council for Gifted and Talented Children
1 South Audley Street
London, WIY 5DQ, England